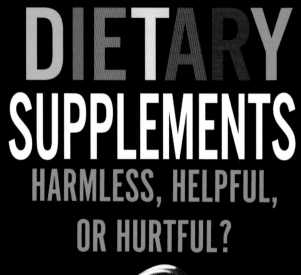

DIETARY SUPPLEMENTS
HARMLESS, HELPFUL, OR HURTFUL?

CONNIE GOLDSMITH

TWENTY-FIRST CENTURY BOOKS / MINNEAPOLIS

Twenty-First Century Books
A division of Lerner Publishing Group, Inc.
241 First Avenue North
Minneapolis, MN 55401 USA

For reading levels and more information, look up this title at www.lernerbooks.com.

Main body text set in Officina Serif ITC Std 10/14.
Typeface provided by International Typeface Corporation

Library of Congress Cataloging-in-Publication Data

Goldsmith, Connie, 1945
    Dietary supplements : harmless, helpful, or hurtful? / by Connie Goldsmith.
        pages cm
    Includes bibliographical references and index.
    ISBN 978-1-4677-3848-4 (lib. bdg. : alk. paper)
    ISBN 978-1-4677-8801-4 (EB pdf)
    1. Dietary supplements—Juvenile literature. I. Title.
    RM258.5.G65 2016
    615.1—dc23   2014024851

Manufactured in the United States of America
1 – VP – 7/15/15

CONTENTS

CHAPTER ONE

WHAT ARE DIETARY SUPPLEMENTS?

> SUPPLEMENTS AREN'T INTENDED TO BE A FOOD SUBSTITUTE BECAUSE THEY CAN'T REPLICATE ALL OF THE NUTRIENTS AND BENEFITS OF WHOLE FOODS, SUCH AS FRUITS AND VEGETABLES. SO DEPENDING ON YOUR SITUATION AND YOUR EATING HABITS, DIETARY SUPPLEMENTS MAY NOT BE WORTH THE EXPENSE.
> —MAYO CLINIC, 2013

MAGGIE DEWOLFE HAS BEEN FIGHTING HER WEIGHT MOST OF HER LIFE. She was just five years old when another little girl told her she was fat. "I was old enough to know that fat meant ugly, so from then on, I was acutely aware of my body." By second grade, bullies began calling her names and insulting her. Boys chased her around the playground and threw rocks at her. "Once I got to high school, I started experimenting with yo-yo diets and weight loss pills to no avail."

After many failed diets, Maggie decided to try a weight-loss supplement. "I'd seen ads for it and thought it would be a quick-fix solution." The supplement Maggie chose contained several herbs, caffeine, and green coffee bean extract.

The first few days, the supplement gave her diarrhea and made her urinate a lot. According to printed information that came with the supplement, this reaction was to be expected as the body got rid of its toxins. Maggie felt better after a few days, but "after a week, the real fun began: I had dizzy spells, constant severe stomach cramps, and headaches, which caused me to miss work and school. The last day I took the [supplement], I had what can only be described as violent vomiting and diarrhea and a high fever," she remembers. "It was an awful experience."

DIETARY SUPPLEMENTS ARE **BIG BUSINESS**

Online sites, TV infomercials, magazine ads, and celebrity tweets make an astonishing array of claims about the improvement to health and performance from dietary supplements. Many promise quick weight loss without dieting. Others promise to build up muscles in just days or to achieve top athletic condition and performance without breaking a sweat. Still others assure users they will be able to stay alert and study harder if they use the supplements.

"Is there really a magic pill that can do it all?"

Do these claims sound good to you? Is there really a magic pill that can do it all?

If you take dietary supplements, you're not alone. The majority of Americans take at least one dietary supplement every day. Many people take half a dozen or more. Supplements promote everything from better health to speedy weight loss and increased strength. "There are at least 50,000 dietary supplements available containing vitamins and minerals, herbs and botanicals, and other ingredients," Dr. Paul Coates of the National Institutes of Health says. "Yet for many of these dietary supplements, there are questions about their effectiveness and safety."

All the same, Americans spend an estimated $32 billion each year on dietary supplements. With that much money at stake, it's not surprising that the powerful dietary supplement industry spent more than $3.6 million in 2013 lobbying Congress to keep government control of the products at a minimum. In addition, the industry contributed more than $703,000 directly to members of Congress the year before, hoping to influence politicians to favor the industry when voting on regulations affecting dietary supplements.

DIETARY SUPPLEMENTS AND HEALTH

Does taking a dietary supplement make people healthier? Or do healthier people take dietary supplements? A 2014 report in the *Nutrition Journal* supports the latter. The article found that "dietary supplement users are more likely than nonusers to adopt a number of positive health-related habits. These include better dietary patterns, exercising regularly, maintaining a healthy body weight, and avoidance of tobacco products." The evidence suggests that users of dietary supplements are seeking wellness and are adopting healthy lifestyle habits as well. Good habits lead to good health. Many experts and medical professionals believe that it is not necessary to take dietary supplements to maintain good health.

DIETARY SUPPLEMENTS AND THE FDA

Our diet is the total of the food and drink we take in on a daily basis. Dietary supplements are products that contain ingredients to add to our diet. They do not replace anything we eat or drink. Dietary supplements include vitamins, minerals, herbs and other botanicals (materials from plants), amino acids (chemicals that help build protein), and enzymes (substances produced by the body to trigger chemical reactions). Dietary supplements come in tablets, capsules, liquids, and powders.

The US Food and Drug Administration (FDA) is the government agency that oversees and regulates a wide range of medical products, foods, prescription drugs, and over-the-counter (OTC) medications. For many products, such as prescription drugs and OTC medications, the agency has strict rules for testing and preapproval before an item ever reaches the market. But the FDA is not tasked with preapproving dietary supplements. The agency has oversight authority only after these products are on the market and available for sale. For this reason, some companies may sell products that are contaminated or that contain untested, illegal, and even dangerous substances.

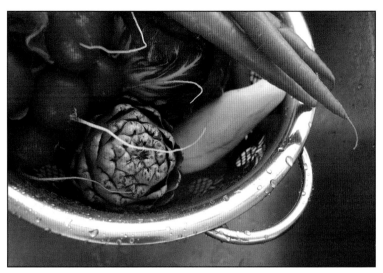

Fruits and vegetables provide many of the vitamins and minerals that people need. Some people worry they don't get enough vitamins and minerals in the food they eat. They may take dietary supplements, even though some experts say supplements are not necessary if you eat a well-balanced diet.

For example, from fall 2013 to spring 2014, nearly one hundred people suffered liver failure from a popular fat-burning supplement. Three people who took the drug required liver transplants and one died. While investigating the cases of liver failure, the FDA discovered the product contained the illegal substance aegeline. The FDA does have legal authority to remove products like this one from the market when they are known to be dangerous, so the agency asked the company to withdraw its aegeline-based supplement from the market. After receiving reports of liver problems, seizures, and muscle damage, the FDA also recalled the dietary supplement that Maggie DeWolfe had taken.

Although the FDA does not officially approve supplements, it does regulate labeling and packaging. Legally, companies that manufacture and sell dietary supplements cannot claim that the products treat or cure an illness or a disease. Only companies that produce medications officially approved by the FDA can make such claims. For this reason, supplement manufacturers can only make general claims about the link between their product and the diseases and health-related conditions they claim to treat. These claims usually describe how dietary supplements affect the structure or the function of the body and suggest that using the supplements will improve health.

For example, the label for a supplement containing calcium and vitamin D can say, "Helps support bone and immune system health." A label for a bottle of vitamin B tablets may say, "Essential for the maintenance of a healthy nervous system." But by law, such

DO IT RIGHT: READ THE LABEL

The FDA requires labels for all dietary supplements to show consumers that the products are supplements. Labels must provide a complete list of ingredients. Labels must define a serving size. The label below, from a multivitamin, must also show the name of each vitamin in the tablets and how much of each is in one serving. (The FDA cannot control the amount of any particular nutrient in any dietary supplement, however.) All other ingredients must also be listed at the bottom of the label. In these multivitamins, the additives include coloring (FD&C Yellow No. 6) and preservatives. Gelatin holds the product together in a gelcap or tablet.

Supplement Facts

Serving Size 1 Tablet

Amount Per Serving		% Daily Value for Children Under 4 Years of Age	% Daily Value for Adults and Children 4 or more Years of Age
Calories	5		
Total Carbohydrate	1 g	†	< 1%*
Sugars	1 g	†	†
Vitamin A	2500 IU	100%	50%
(50% as beta-carotene)			
Vitamin C	40 mg	100%	67%
Vitamin D	400 IU	100%	100%
Vitamin E	15 IU	150%	50%
Thiamin	1.1 mg	157%	73%
Riboflavin	1.2 mg	150%	71%
Niacin	14 mg	156%	70%
Vitamin B6	1.1 mg	157%	55%
Folate	300 mcg	150%	75%
Vitamin B12	5 mcg	167%	83%

* Percent Daily Values are based on a 2,000 calorie diet.
† Daily Value not established.

Other ingredients: Sucrose, sodium ascorbate, stearic acid, gelatin, maltodextrins, artificial flavors, dl-alpha tocopheryl acetate, niacinamide, magnesium stearate, Yellow 6, artificial colors, stearic acid, palmitic acid, pyridoxine hydrochloride, thiamin mononitrate, vitamin A acetate, beta-carotene, folic acid, cholecalciferol, and cyanocobalamin.

← The label clearly states the product is a supplement.

← The label defines a serving as one tablet size.

← The label lists each ingredient and the amount in each serving.

← Other ingredients: flavorings, coloring, and preservatives wording also requires a disclaimer, or a statement of explanation. The disclaimer for a dietary supplement must appear on the label and must say, "This statement has not been evaluated by the Food and Drug Administration. This product is not intended to diagnose, treat, cure, or prevent any disease." Precisely because supplements are not preapproved by the FDA, experts always advise consumers to check with trusted health-care professionals before deciding to take any of these products.

WHO WATCHES OUT FOR **SUPPLEMENT SAFETY?**

If so many Americans use dietary supplements, why doesn't the FDA regulate them in the same way it regulates drugs and medications? Before 1994 dietary supplements were subject to the same FDA regulations as medications, which require extensive testing before a product is approved for sale. That year Senators Orrin Hatch of Utah and Tom Harkin of Iowa introduced the Dietary Supplement Health and Education Act (DSHEA) of 1994.

The act became law, shifting dietary supplements out of the category of drugs to that of foods, which are subject to less strict regulations. Many Americans viewed the new law as a victory since it ensures that the FDA can monitor product labeling and packaging, take legal action against unsafe products, and require basic manufacturing standards of quality. But many critics viewed the shift as a dangerous weakening of safety standards. For example, Dr. Pieter Cohen of Harvard Medical School says the consequence of DSHEA is that "the FDA is charged with the unenviable task of identifying and removing dangerous supplements only after they have caused harm."

Supplements are not exactly food or medicines. Instead, they fall into an unregulated black hole. Under DSHEA the company that makes a dietary supplement is responsible for ensuring its safety before selling it. The manufacturer is also responsible for the truthfulness of health claims on the product label. Yet many critics wonder if companies that make their money selling supplements can or should be allowed to police themselves.

"There's no requirement for a company making a dietary supplement to seek FDA approval or to provide evidence that the product is safe and effective for its intended uses," says Dr. Michael Carome, director of a consumer protection organization. "There's no FDA review of evidence related to clinical trials that might have tested the product."

When consumers and health-care providers become aware of health risks or dangers associated with the use of a supplement, they may report those problems directly to the FDA at http://www.fda.gov /medwatch or by calling (800) 332-1088. They may also contact the manufacturer directly. In the past, makers of dietary supplements reported consumer and health-care provider complaints to the FDA only on a voluntary basis. As of December 2007, manufacturers are required to notify the FDA of such complaints within fifteen days. The FDA studies the information to determine if a product is a risk to the public. If the FDA finds a supplement may be harmful, it can restrict the product's use, seize the product, or remove it from the marketplace entirely.

The FDA can also take action if a supplement makes false claims. For example, in January 2014, the FDA sent a warning letter to an Oregon supplement manufacturer that claimed its supplements treat cancer and heart disease. The company also said its products can prevent radiation sickness and related death. This claim preys on the ongoing fears among some Americans—particularly those on the West Coast—of the risk of radiation exposure from the 2011 Fukushima nuclear disaster in Japan. The FDA warned that failure to correct the labeling violations would lead to legal action.

BEFORE 1994 . . .

Before a company makes and sells a new supplement, it must notify the FDA if it plans to market a supplement with an ingredient not used before DSHEA became law in 1994. Then, under the DSHEA law, the manufacturer must demonstrate to the FDA that the new ingredient is safe to use. However, neither the government nor the dietary supplement industry maintains an official list of dietary ingredients marketed before 1994. Therefore, the manufacturers themselves are responsible for determining if a dietary ingredient is new and whether it requires FDA approval. As a result, supplement manufacturers seldom seek FDA approval prior to marketing a new supplement, and the FDA cannot strictly enforce this part of the DSHEA law.

FINDING **SAFER** SUPPLEMENTS

Independent organizations, such as ConsumerLab.com (CL), NSF International, and the U.S. Pharmacopeial (USP) Convention offer seals of approval that may be displayed on dietary supplements. These seals mean that the product has passed the organization's quality tests for measures such as potency and for the presence or absence of contaminants. This does not mean the product is effective, however. It means the product was properly manufactured, that it contains the ingredients listed on the label, and that it does not contain harmful levels of contaminants.

- CL tests ensure that products contain the amount of ingredient claimed on the label and that the product is free of contaminants. CL randomly retests the products every twelve months.

- "NSF certification on a product means the product complies with all standard requirements. NSF conducts periodic unannounced inspections and product testing to verify that the product continues to comply with the standards."

- "The USP Convention Verified Mark is awarded to dietary supplement products that successfully undergo and meet the stringent requirements of its voluntary USP Dietary Supplement Verification Process."

IS THIS SUPPLEMENT **FOR ME?**

There is little scientific evidence to support the need for many common dietary supplements. Risks very often outweigh the benefits. Before taking a dietary supplement, always talk to a health-care professional. Questions to consider include the following:

- Can this product help me?
- Is it safe?
- How much should I take?
- How long should I take it?

Experts urge caution when taking dietary supplements. Many experts suggest avoiding them altogether. "Speed up your body naturally," says Jill Koegel, registered dietitian and certified personal trainer. "Don't do it with a chemical that isn't regulated and that we don't understand. It doesn't make sense. Taking supplements to satisfy the desire for a perfect body or to accomplish superhuman performance causes severe illnesses and deaths over and over, yet people continue to watch for the next pill or powder to try."

CHAPTER TWO

WHAT'S ON YOUR PLATE?

FOOD IS ALWAYS THE BEST WAY FOR PEOPLE TO GET ALL THE
VITAMINS AND MINERALS THEY NEED. THE LESS PROCESSED THE
FOOD, THE MORE NUTRITIOUS IT IS. WHOLE FOODS ALSO CONTAIN
OTHER SUBSTANCES THAT KEEP US HEALTHY.
—DALE AMES KLINE, REGISTERED DIETITIAN, 2014

**MANDY MARTIN STARTED PUTTING ON WEIGHT WHEN SHE TOOK
A JOB WHERE SHE HAD TO SIT DURING HER ENTIRE THIRTEEN-
HOUR SHIFT.** And on her way home, she often stopped at a gas station
for a supersized burrito nicknamed the Bomb. It wasn't long before
Mandy put on 40 pounds (18 kilograms). She started a string of fad
diets but didn't stick to them on the weekends. One day Mandy saw a
picture of herself that shocked her. "I was stunned that I looked that
bad. That was my wake-up call to do something for real."

Mandy left convenience store food behind and went grocery
shopping. She stocked up on whole grains, lean meats, and produce.
In five months of healthy eating, she lost 20 pounds (9 kg). Then she
took it to the next level by adding exercise to her daily routine. "At first
I couldn't walk on the treadmill for more than five minutes," she says. "I
worked up to 30 minutes of walking and running." She lost 10 pounds
(4.5 kg). Soon she added weight lifting to her workout and lost another
20 pounds.

Mandy once weighed 185 pounds (84 kg). After she added healthy eating and exercise to her life, her weight dropped to 133 pounds (60 kg). She moved to Colorado to study sports medicine and has a new career as a personal trainer. Mandy has this tip for grocery shopping. "The food you need most—fresh produce—is around the edges of the grocery store, not in the middle."

PACKING ON **THE POUNDS**

What did you have for lunch last Saturday? A double cheeseburger and onion rings? Two slices of pepperoni pizza? A basket of hot wings and fries from the food court? Maybe all washed down with a supersized soda or frozen drink? Your taste buds may thank you but the rest of your body, not so much.

Teen obesity has quadrupled over the past thirty years. More than one-third of children and adolescents are overweight or obese. An estimated 69 percent of adults are overweight or obese. According to the Centers for Disease Control and Prevention (CDC), "*Overweight* is defined as having excess body weight for a particular height from fat, muscle, bone, water, or a combination of these factors. *Obesity* is defined as having excess body fat."

People who are overweight and obese eat too many calories. Often they're also eating too few nutrients—the substances in food that provide nourishment for growth and health. Some families cannot afford to buy fresh fruits and vegetables and other healthy foods. More often people can afford to eat well but may not understand what makes up a healthy diet or why it is so important. Instead, they eat unhealthy foods that are high in sugar and fat and that can pack on the pounds.

> **More than one-third of American children and adolescents are overweight or obese.**

HOW MANY CALORIES DO I NEED?

The US government's Office of Disease Prevention and Health Promotion offers these guidelines for the estimated daily calorie needs by age, gender, and activity level.

AGE/GENDER	SEDENTARY	MODERATELY ACTIVE	ACTIVE
12-year-old boy	1,800	2,200	2,400
14-year-old boy	2,000	2,400	2,800
16- to 18-year-old boy	2,400	2,800	3,200
12-year-old girl	1,600	2,000	2,200
14- to 18-year-old girl	1,800	2,000	2,400

DOES THIS FOOD MAKE ME LOOK FAT?

Knowing more about healthy eating makes it easier to understand the world of dietary supplements and their hyped-up promises. All food is divided into three groups: carbohydrates (carbs), protein, and fat. These three groups are also called macronutrients (*macro* means "big") because they are the big, important foundations of a healthy diet. (Vitamins and minerals are micronutrients.)

Carbs are found in many foods in the form of sugar, starch, and fiber. Carbs provide the ready energy we need for our daily activities. Healthy sources of carbs include fresh or frozen fruits, vegetables, and whole grains. Animal products (such as meat, fish, eggs, and milk), certain vegetables (such as beans and lentils), and seeds and nuts contain the protein we need to build and maintain our bodies. Fats come from animal products (such as butter and meat) and from plants (such as avocados and the oil from olives). Small amounts of fat provide energy, help vitamin absorption, insulate the body, and help body systems function correctly.

A teaspoon of protein has the same number of calories as a teaspoon of carbs. A teaspoon of fat has more than twice the calories as the same amount of protein and of carbs. Some people worry about eating too many carbs, thinking they lead to weight gain. Others agonize over fats. But none of the macronutrients are inherently bad for you (unless you have an unusual medical condition). Optimal health is all about choosing the right amounts of these necessary food groups.

To help you make the best decisions, the US Department of Agriculture (USDA) recommends that teens eat 1.5 to 2 cups of fruits and 2.5 to 3 cups of vegetables each day. Add 6 to 8 ounces (170 to 227 grams) of grain products and 5.5 to 6 ounces (156 to 170 g) of protein. Top it off with 3 cups of milk and other dairy products for a healthy daily diet.

AIM FOR A HEALTHY LIFESTYLE

It's no secret that poor diet and physical inactivity are the main causes of the American obesity epidemic. Overweight and obese children and teens are much more likely to become overweight and obese adults. Nearly two-thirds of obese adolescents will become obese adults, even if their parents are not obese. And eight out of ten obese ten- to fourteen-year-olds who have an obese parent will become obese adults. The CDC Body Mass Index Calculator for Child and Teen at http://nccd .cdc.gov/dnpabmi/ is a great way to discover if you are at a healthy weight. The CDC recommends consulting a health-care provider about your results.

Obese teens are more likely to have risk factors for heart disease, such as high cholesterol or high blood pressure. One study of obese five- to seventeen-year-olds found 70 percent had at least one risk factor for heart disease. Being overweight or obese also puts people at risk for type 2 diabetes, asthma, arthritis, and sleep apnea, as well

DO IT RIGHT: MAKE YOUR PLATE A HEALTHY PLATE

ChooseMyPlate *(logo at right)* was developed by the USDA to help Americans balance meals. The program is intended to help people think about building a healthy plate of food at mealtimes.

Fruits and vegetables should fill half your plate, with grains and protein taking up the rest. At least half your grains should be whole grains, such as whole wheat, oatmeal, or brown rice. Vary protein choices. Choose lean meats, poultry, seafood, beans and peas, and nuts and seeds. A serving of nonfat or 1 percent fat milk completes the meal.

as cancers of the breast, colon, kidney, thyroid, and prostate. Teens who are overweight or obese may also develop poor self-esteem and experience bullying.

Most people who become overweight or obese simply eat more calories than they burn up. The reasons for overeating are complex. A person may have difficulty judging a healthy serving size or may simply prefer high-fat or high-sugar foods. And because teens are busy with school, homework, sports, activities with family and friends, and after-school jobs, it can be hard to make the time to eat right. A teen may, instead, choose an easy, quick meal of high-calorie, high-fat foods from a fast-food restaurant.

Reputable websites and publications from government and health organizations provide helpful information on healthy diets. The ChooseMyPlate.gov site is sponsored by the USDA and offers tips on healthy eating for an active teen lifestyle. The site helps answer the question, What is the best way to make the right choices? Here are basic guidelines:

- *Load up with nutrient-packed foods.* Eat nutrient-dense foods including whole grains, lean protein, fruits and vegetables, and low-fat or nonfat dairy products such as milk or yogurt. Eat less sugar, salt, and solid fats overall. Liquid oils such as olive or canola oil are healthier than solid fats such as butter or margarine.
- *Energize with grains.* Bread, pasta, cereals, and tortillas supply quick energy to your body. Be sure at least half the grain you eat is whole grain, such as brown rice, whole-wheat bread, and oatmeal. Processed grains, such as white rice and white flour, are less nutritious.
- *Power up with protein.* Protein repairs and builds muscles. Choose lean or low-fat cuts of meat such as skinless chicken and turkey. Get your protein from seafood twice a week. Selecting canned tuna and salmon packed in water is an affordable way to eat seafood.
- *Mix it up with plant proteins.* Plants are a great source of protein too. Choose beans, peas, and legumes. They are relatively low in calories and keep you feeling full for several hours. Soy

products are high in protein as well. Unsalted nuts and seeds also are good sources of protein.

- *Vary your fruits and vegetables for maximum nutrition.* Eat a rainbow of fruits and vegetables every day: blueberries, blackberries, raspberries, strawberries; red and yellow peppers; and salads with dark greens such as spinach and kale. The varied colors of vegetables and fruits represent a wide variety of nutrients called phytochemicals. Scientists believe produce may have as many as four thousand phytochemicals, such as beta-carotene, lycopene, and lutein. Each of these nutrients helps your body in different ways. Remember too that fresh may taste better, but frozen and canned vegetables and fruits are often less expensive and have similar nutrients. Read the labels to make sure packaged fruits and vegetables do not have added sugar or salt.
- *Don't forget dairy.* Fat-free and low-fat dairy products help to build and maintain bones, which is especially important for growing teens. Consider milk, yogurt, and cheese. People who can't eat dairy foods may be able to substitute calcium-fortified soy, almond, and rice milk.
- *Drink water.* Skip the sugary soft drinks and high-fat lattes. Stay hydrated by drinking plain water instead. Keep a reusable water bottle nearby so you always have water with you. Boys need about 14 cups (3.3 liters) of total fluids per day, while girls need about 10 cups (2.3 liters). Most of the fluid intake should be plain water.

STAYING ACTIVE

For some people, it can be harder to stay active than it is to eat right. According to the American Academy of Pediatrics, teens spend about eleven hours each day plugged into electronic media, such as television, computers, tablets, and smartphones. Some of that time is for schoolwork, but much of it is purely social. For a healthier lifestyle, sign off for an hour and play ball, jog, go for a walk, or ride a bike.

Not only does exercise make you feel and look better, one study showed that kids who started exercising in middle school earned better

To improve health, join a fitness group. Exercising with friends can be fun! Try something that's new to you, such as yoga or Latin dance.

grades in high school. Medical experts recommend that teens get sixty minutes of moderate to vigorous physical activity each day. Yet a 2014 government report found that only one-fourth of high school students get the recommended amount of daily exercise.

No need to despair if you're a couch potato in training. There are many ways to increase physical activity. Start slowly. Walk the dog or walk with a friend if you don't have a dog. Give yoga a try. You can start with an inexpensive yoga mat and a free YouTube video or a DVD borrowed from your library. Community centers often offer inexpensive yoga and exercise classes. Or get into exergaming. You can burn way more calories when exergaming than when playing a sit-down video game.

As you get more energy, join your best friend in another, more energetic activity you both like. Take a hike. Ride a bike. Play volleyball at the beach. Swim at the local pool. Hit the gym. Team up with a partner who is as dedicated to exercise as you are. Research shows that if you pair up for exercise, you're more likely to stay with it long term. You can do it!

Another way to build long-term success is to download an app to track your nutrition and exercise programs. Earn recognition for meeting your healthy eating and physical activity goals by signing up for the Presidential Active Lifestyle Award at http://www.presidentschallenge.org.

CHAPTER THREE

VITAMINS AND MINERALS

THE SUPPLEMENT INDUSTRY IS A BOOMING BUSINESS. THEIR POWERFUL ADVERTISEMENTS CAN EASILY CONVINCE ATHLETES THAT VITAMIN AND MINERAL PILLS WILL ENHANCE SPORTS PERFORMANCE. YET, THERE IS LITTLE SCIENTIFIC EVIDENCE TO SUPPORT THOSE CLAIMS.
—NANCY CLARK, REGISTERED DIETITIAN AND MEMBER OF THE AMERICAN COLLEGE OF SPORTS MEDICINE, 2014

CINDY COTTE GRIFFITHS, A YOGA INSTRUCTOR LIVING IN MARYLAND, SEEMED TO BE IN EXCELLENT HEALTH. But something was wrong. "Many of my family and friends who spent time with me knew that I'd been suffering from bone and muscle pain but resisted going to a doctor," she says. "At times the pain was so severe in my shoulders and arms it prevented my normal physical activities. At first I thought I'd overdone it with my fitness routine, even though the pain arrived on a morning after two days of rest."

Then things got even worse. Cindy's muscles grew weak. She went to her doctor who ordered a series of blood tests. He discovered a severe vitamin D deficiency. "Vitamin D helps the body control calcium and phosphate levels," Cindy says. "If the blood levels of these minerals become too low, the body may produce hormones that cause calcium and phosphate to be released from the bones, causing weak bones. Researchers estimate 50% of the world's population may be at risk."

"Vitamins and minerals are micronutrients—we need only small amounts of them for good health."

At first, Cindy wondered how this could happen to her. Then she realized she used to run outside in the sunshine five times a week. When she began spending more time indoors at yoga sessions, she wasn't getting enough vitamin D. "Fifteen minutes a day in the sun is all you need to acquire enough vitamin D in your body," she says.

Cindy checked out the food and drinks in her kitchen. She realized her family was getting plenty of calcium in milk and fortified orange juice but only half of the vitamin D they needed. "I'm sharing my story because taking a supplement is an easy fix and the complications from not treating the deficiency can be quite dire including high blood pressure, obesity, osteoporosis, and early mortality."

Cindy reminds people to think about their vitamin D intake. "Are you getting enough? Make sure you are—especially in the winter when we aren't outside as much and tend to stay warm under layers of clothing. My doctor prescribed a supplement for the next 24 weeks. Hopefully I'll be feeling better soon."

EAT YOUR CARROTS

All your life, you've probably heard about vitamins and minerals—and the fruits and vegetables that are loaded with them. "Eat your broccoli. It's full of vitamins." Or "Eat your carrots. They're good for your eyes." And "Drink your milk. It builds strong bones." All are true. But what exactly are vitamins and minerals?

Vitamins, such as A, B, and C, are nutrients found naturally in almost all foods. Minerals, such as iron and calcium, are also found in many foods. Vitamins and minerals are micronutrients—we need only small amounts of them for good health. Unlike macronutrients (carbohydrates, protein, and fat), which contain calories, vitamins and minerals do not contain calories nor do they provide energy to your body.

Orange vegetables, such as carrots and yams, are high in vitamin A and can benefit vision.

Once you absorb vitamins and minerals from food or dietary supplements, your body uses them in many ways, including metabolism and energy production. According to the Mayo Clinic, "Metabolism is the process by which your body converts what you eat and drink into energy. During this complex biochemical process, calories in food and beverages are combined with oxygen to release the energy your body needs to function. Even when you're at rest, your body needs energy for all its 'hidden' functions, such as breathing, circulating blood, adjusting hormone levels, and growing and repairing cells."

THE ABCs OF VITAMINS

One in two adult Americans pops a daily multivitamin pill in the belief it improves or maintains health. And millions of parents give chewable vitamins or "gummy" vitamins to their children. In fact, the multivitamin industry is a $12 billion business. But do vitamins and minerals really make people healthier—or are they a waste of money? Humans require thirteen vitamins—A, C, D, E, K, and eight different B vitamins—for optimal health. While food can provide all the vitamins we need, food manufacturers are sometimes legally required to add extra vitamins to many foods such as cereal, bread, juice, and milk. These foods are vitamin fortified, and they help us get enough of the vitamins we need in our daily diet. We need the following thirteen vitamins:

- *Vitamin A* is important for maintaining healthy vision and a strong immune system. It helps the heart, lungs, kidneys, and other organs work properly. It's found naturally in leafy green vegetables such as spinach and kale. It is also in other green, orange, and yellow vegetables and fruits such as broccoli, carrots, yams, and apricots. Fish—especially salmon—is another great source of vitamin A.

- *The eight B vitamins* include thiamine, riboflavin, niacin, pantothenic acid, biotin, B-6, B-12, and folate. Each B vitamin is chemically distinct, and all are important to bodily functions such as metabolism. These vitamins are found naturally in a variety of meats (especially turkey), fruits, vegetables, and whole grains. However, many B vitamins are lost in processing, for example, when wheat is turned into white flour. By law, thiamine, riboflavin, niacin, and folic acid must be added back to white flour before manufacturers can sell it.

- *Vitamin B-12* helps to keep nerve and blood cells healthy. It's also vital to the formation of deoxyribonucleic acid (DNA) in our cells. DNA carries the genetic code that makes us who we are. Too little vitamin B-12 can lead to anemia—a shortage of oxygen-carrying red blood cells—that may leave a person feeling weak and tired. Vitamin B-12 is found exclusively in animal foods such as fish, meat, poultry, eggs, and milk. Vegans, who eat no animal products, or vegetarians, who eat some but not all animal products, should consult with a health-care provider to see if they need to take a B-12 supplement or to eat larger amounts of B-12 fortified foods.

- *Folate* is a B vitamin the body uses in cellular division. It's necessary for the ongoing creation of DNA in our new cells. It's found naturally in many dark leafy greens, broccoli and other vegetables; in citrus fruits; in nuts; and in legumes such as peanuts and kidney beans. Manufacturers often add folate to processed grain products. Doctors may prescribe folic acid, a form of folate, for pregnant women to ensure healthy fetal development.

- *Vitamin C* (also called ascorbic acid) is a natural antioxidant—a substance that helps to protect the body from cell damage. Vitamin C assists the body's immune system to work properly and helps the body make the connective tissue known as collagen. Citrus fruits, berries, and fruit juices are good natural sources of vitamin C as are vegetables such as potatoes and tomatoes.
- *Vitamin D* supports bone health by promoting the body's ability to absorb calcium from food. Muscles, nerves, and the immune system also require vitamin D to function properly. Exposure to as little as ten to fifteen minutes of sunlight each day naturally creates vitamin D for fair-skinned individuals. People with darker skin need up to six times more sun exposure to make the same amount of vitamin D. Other naturally occurring sources of this vitamin are fatty fish such as salmon and tuna, cheeses, and eggs. Much of the vitamin D in American diets comes from fortified foods such as packaged cereals, orange juice, and milk. Read labels to see which foods are fortified with this important vitamin.
- *Vitamin E* is an antioxidant. It boosts the body's immune system and helps to keep blood from clotting. Vitamin E is found naturally in vegetable oils, nuts, seeds, and green vegetables such as broccoli and spinach. We get some of our vitamin E from fortified foods such as margarine, breakfast cereals, and juices.
- *Vitamin K* helps blood to clot properly and is found naturally in leafy green vegetables such as spinach, asparagus, cabbage, and celery.

It's important to get the right amount of vitamins in our daily diets. But too much of any vitamin can actually be unhealthy or even harmful. For example, too much vitamin A can cause dizziness, blurred vision, and birth defects. Excessive amounts of vitamins E and K can interfere with blood clotting and with prescription blood thinners.

Always consult with a doctor before taking any vitamins and to determine a safe dosage.

MINERALS ROCK

Do you ever play twenty questions? The first question is, "Is it animal, vegetable, or mineral?" Unlike animals and vegetables, minerals are not living organisms. Examples of minerals include iron, magnesium, and zinc. Minerals are found naturally in the earth. Plants take in minerals from the soil as they grow. Animals get minerals from eating those plants. Humans obtain minerals from eating plants and from eating animals that have eaten mineral-containing plants.

For humans and animals, minerals are necessary for strong bones and teeth. Minerals also control the movement of body fluids inside and outside of cells and help turn food into energy. Minerals important for human health include the following:

- *Calcium* is used to build and maintain strong bones and teeth. Calcium also helps the heart, muscles, and nerves function correctly. Many young people don't get enough calcium. When the body doesn't get adequate calcium, it takes what it needs from the bones so the heart, nerves, and muscles can continue to function well. Over the long term, calcium deficiency may result in osteoporosis, which leads to bone loss and fractures. Americans' primary sources of calcium are milk, cheese, and yogurt. Some dark green vegetables such as spinach and broccoli contain smaller amounts of calcium. Packaged foods such as orange juice and cereals often contain added calcium.
- *Iron* is a component of hemoglobin, the protein in red blood cells that carries oxygen from the lungs throughout the body. Iron helps the body make many other proteins and enzymes needed for good health. Meat, poultry, and fish provide much of our iron. Nonanimal sources of iron include soybeans, lentils, beans, and iron-fortified foods such as breakfast cereals and breads. Labels will tell you whether a food product is iron fortified.
- *Sodium and potassium* help nerves and muscles work correctly. Sodium also balances body fluids. Potassium helps to move

nutrients into cells and waste products out of cells. It also offsets sodium's tendency to increase blood pressure. Eating a variety of fruits and vegetables generally provides all the potassium people need. Bananas, cantaloupe, sweet potatoes, and winter squash, for example, are all excellent natural sources of potassium. Most Americans get more than enough sodium in their diets from processed foods and from adding salt to foods. Healthy people seldom need to take extra sodium or potassium supplements.

- *Other minerals* important to good health include phosphorus, magnesium, sulfur, iron, zinc, manganese, copper, iodine, cobalt, fluoride, and selenium. Eating a variety of different foods—including fruits, vegetables, dairy, lean meats, and grains—generally provides the small amounts of these minerals needed for good health. Ask your doctor or another trusted medical professional if you have questions.

TO TAKE OR **NOT TO TAKE?**

Millions of Americans young and old take supplements, believing they are an essential element of maintaining good health. Yet many doctors say that scientific research overwhelmingly shows that the majority of healthy people don't need to take vitamins and minerals at all. In a 2013 study published in the prestigious *Annals of Internal Medicine,* a group of doctors said, "The message is simple: Most supplements do not prevent chronic disease or death, their use is not justified, and they should be avoided. This message is especially true for the general population with no clear evidence of micronutrient deficiencies, who represent most supplement users in the United States and in other countries."

Is it ever necessary to take vitamin and mineral supplements? In some cases, yes. Certain diseases and medical conditions such as cancer or stomach surgery that disrupt normal digestion can lead to vitamin or mineral deficiencies. "There are times when extra vitamins and minerals are used to treat specific health conditions," says Dale Ames Kline, a leading registered dietitian and author. "The use of these supplemental nutrients should be based on medical need. People

DO IT RIGHT: SELECTED RECOMMENDED DIETARY ALLOWANCES FOR TEENS (14–18)

The Recommended Dietary Allowance (RDA) is the daily amount of a nutrient sufficient to meet the requirements of 97 to 98 percent of healthy people. The RDA varies by age, gender, and whether a woman is pregnant or breastfeeding. For more information about teen nutrition, check out Teens Health from Nemours, one of the largest nonprofit organizations devoted to young people's health at http://kidshealth.org/teen/. Click on Food & Fitness on the left, then Nutrition Basics in the middle. You'll find dozens of helpful articles about vitamins, minerals, and how to stick to a healthy diet. Below are a few RDA recommendations for teens:

NUTRIENT	MALE	FEMALE	FOOD SOURCE (approx. amount)
Vitamin A	900 mcg*	700 mcg	A medium carrot
Vitamin C	75 mg*	65 mg	A small orange
Thiamine	1.2 mg	1.0 mg	A 3-ounce (85g) pork chop and 1/4 cup of macadamia nuts
Niacin	16 mg	14 mg	3 ounces of chicken or turkey breast and 1/4 cup of peanuts
Calcium	1300 mg	1300 mg	2 cups milk, 1 cup yogurt, and 1.5 ounces (43g) cheese
Iron	11 mg	15 mg	6 to 7 ounces (170 to 198g) beef and 3 ounces dark chocolate; OR 1 cup cereal fortified with 100 percent RDA iron

*(mcg = micrograms; mg = milligrams)

with low vitamin D levels may need a supplement. Pregnant women and those trying to become pregnant often need additional folic acid. Seriously ill people may need supplements to prevent malnutrition and to help heal wounds." As with any question about supplements, consult with a doctor or other trusted health-care provider before taking vitamin or mineral supplements.

CHAPTER FOUR

HERBAL SUPPLEMENTS

A LOT OF CONSUMERS HAVE A PRECONCEIVED NOTION THAT IF IT'S A NATURAL PRODUCT, IT MUST BE SAFE. BUT THAT IS NOT NECESSARILY THE CASE. MOST OF THESE PRODUCTS ARE NOT WELL-REGULATED AND HAVE VERY LITTLE OVERSIGHT. TRACES OF HEAVY METALS AND PRESCRIPTION DRUGS HAVE EVEN BEEN FOUND IN SOME HERBAL AND DIETARY SUPPLEMENTS.
—HERBERT BONKOVSKY, MD, AMERICAN COLLEGE OF GASTROENTEROLOGY, 2014

A PHONE CALL WOKE TOM AND KAREN SCHLENDORF OF LONG ISLAND, NEW YORK, EARLY ONE MORNING. The local police department told them that an officer was on the way over with some news. "My blood just went cold as ice," Karen said. "Oh, my God, I hope it's not Pete." Her twenty-year-old son Peter was attending college in Albany, New York. At the time, however, he was on spring break with friends in the beach town of Panama City, Florida. "I'm sorry to have to tell you this," the officer said after greeting them at the door. "Your son is dead."

After talking to Pete's friends, Karen learned they'd spent the day touring the beach town's novelty shops. Flashy signs promoted small packets of herbal supplements guaranteed to deliver increased energy, cosmic consciousness, and inner visions. And they were natural, legal, and cheap. The young men decided on an herbal supplement whose label recommended a four-tablet dose. Most of the young men followed the store clerk's suggestion to take twelve to fifteen tablets instead.

Pete took eight tablets, and that night, he felt too sick to go out with his friends. Instead, he stayed behind at the motel. Several hours later, when Pete's friends returned, they found him dead on the floor. The medical examiner discovered that Peter Schlendorf had died from a lethal overdose of the stimulants ephedrine, pseudoephedrine, phenylpropanolamine, and caffeine—all ingredients in the herbal supplement Pete had taken.

WHAT'S IN YOUR HERBAL SUPPLEMENT?

An estimated twenty thousand herbal products are sold legally in the United States. Nearly one-fifth of American adults take herbal products, according to a study published in the *Journal of General Internal Medicine*. And herbal supplement manufacturers, which earn at least $5 billion from supplement sales each year, make all kinds of fantastic claims about their products. They say their supplements can do everything from relieving stress and anxiety to curing hyperactivity disorders in children and Alzheimer's disease in adults.

Many manufacturers claim to do it with all-natural ingredients. The word *natural* sounds appealing to most Americans. It sounds healthy. What could be wrong with an all-natural product? However, *natural* does not always mean safe. A poisonous mushroom, for example, is all natural. A pie made from rhubarb stalks can be yummy, yet the leaves of the rhubarb plant cause kidney failure and seizures.

As with other dietary supplements, the FDA has no authority to approve herbal supplements before manufacturers market them to the public. Instead, the FDA receives reports of "serious adverse events" (disability, hospitalizations, or death) from health-care providers and consumers. The FDA is responsible for investigating the safety of a supplement only after it receives an adverse event report. The organization received 600 reports of serious adverse events in 2008. It also received about 350 reports of moderate or mild adverse events. The number of all adverse events may be as high as 50,000 each year, the FDA estimates. Many people don't connect their illness or condition to dietary supplements. They believe that most supplements—especially herbal supplements—are safe.

Many of the active ingredients in herbal supplements are actually

Be sure to consult your health-care provider before taking any herbal remedies. Some may help, but others are risky. Still others may interfere with prescription medications.

unknown. An herb may contain dozens or even hundreds of chemicals, making it difficult or impossible to identify which chemical is helpful or hurtful. For example, ginkgo, which people sometimes take to improve memory, contains at least thirty-three different chemical components. The National Center for Complementary and Alternative Medicine (NCCAM)—part of the US government's National Institutes of Health—conducts and supports research to provide information about complementary practices and health products, including herbal remedies. Scientists at NCCAM are working to identify the substances in herbal products.

Yet even when ingredients are known, not all herbal supplements are alike. For example, a tablet of ginkgo from one bottle or manufacturer may not contain the same amount of ginkgo as a tablet from another bottle or manufacturer. Herbal supplements, sometimes called botanicals, are made from the leaves, flowers, seeds, berries, bark, and roots of plants and trees. The plants from which herbal supplements are made are living organisms. Different plants of the same species may differ from one another depending on factors such as the soil in which they grow and how much water and sunlight the plant receives. Differences in manufacturing processes can also lead to varying amounts of the herb in any given tablet. Many herbal supplements sold in the United States are manufactured overseas where the United States has no oversight or regulatory power.

HERBAL TREATMENTS THROUGH HISTORY

In the twenty-first century, herbal supplements are sold in various places, including health food stores, acupuncture clinics, neighborhood gyms, and online. They come in many forms, including fresh or dried plants, tablets and capsules, teas, and powders.

Medicines made from plants can be powerful and effective. Plant-based medicines have been used around the world as legitimate treatments for medical conditions for at least five thousand years. In fact, between one-third and one-half of currently prescribed medications were first derived from plants. For example, the ancient Egyptians and Greeks brewed a tea from willow bark and used it to reduce fever and pain. By the end of the nineteenth century, scientists at the German drug firm Bayer had developed a synthetic form of the chemical and called it aspirin. Additionally, synthetic

Diocorides was a Greek physician, pharmacologist, and botanist. Between 50 and 70 CE, he wrote an encyclopedia called De Materia Medica *about herbal medicine that was widely read for fifteen centuries.*

forms of chemicals found naturally in foxglove plants, cinchona trees, and the Pacific yew are used in the twenty-first century to treat heart disease, malaria, and cancer, respectively.

However, the effectiveness of many plant-based medicines sold as supplements is often not supported by scientific evidence. Supplements such as echinacea and St. John's wort, for example, are popular but haven't been scientifically proven to treat the conditions for which they are marketed. In fact, some supplements can be dangerous to a person's health. Echinacea, for example, may cause allergic reactions, irregular heartbeats, and liver damage. And St. John's wort interacts with a large number of prescription medications (including oral contraceptives) and has been linked to headaches, hives, rashes, and upset stomach.

COMMON HERBAL SUPPLEMENTS

A study published in the *Journal of General Internal Medicine* described the ten most commonly used herbal supplements in the United States, in order of use, and what they are used for. Scientific evidence does not conclusively support the effectiveness of any of them. So consult with a doctor or other trusted medical professional about any herbal supplement you may be considering, especially if you have any known allergies or are taking any prescription medications. The ten most commonly used herbal supplements are the following:

Herb	Common use	Scientific evidence for effectiveness
Echinacea	Colds, flu, strengthen the immune system	Inconclusive
Ginseng	Physical and cognitive performance	Inconclusive
Ginkgo biloba	Dementia and memory loss Leg cramps	Likely effective Likely effective

Herb	Common use	Scientific evidence for effectiveness
Garlic	High cholesterol	Likely effective
St. John's wort	Depression	Likely effective for mild to moderate depression
Peppermint	Upset stomach, irritable bowel syndrome	Inconclusive
Ginger	Nausea	Inconclusive
Soy	Menopausal symptoms High cholesterol	Not effective Effective
Chamomile	Insomnia, stomach problems	No high-quality data
Kava-kava	Anxiety Insomnia	Likely effective Inconclusive

Other widely used herbal remedies include flaxseed, milk thistle, and valerian. According to the NCCAM, people take flaxseed or flaxseed oil to lower cholesterol, to manage heart disease, and to prevent cancer. Flaxseed may help lower cholesterol in some people, but there is not enough scientific evidence to support its use for any of those purposes. NCCAM is funding studies of flaxseed to learn more about how the plant impacts these conditions.

Milk thistle is typically used for liver disorders. Some research shows it may be effective for liver disease caused by alcohol abuse, but other studies show no improvement. Valerian, used for insomnia, is one of the few herbal remedies that has been scientifically studied. However, studies show mixed results. Some studies suggest it helps short-term insomnia, while other study results are inconclusive.

GROWING DEMAND

An estimated three-quarters of the world's population have used or are using some type of herbal supplement, and the demand for safe, reliable herbal remedies is increasing in the United States, Canada, Europe, and India. This is particularly true among people who turn to complementary, or integrative, care. This care combines standard medical care with practices such as herbal medicine, massage, meditation, and acupuncture to manage a range of physical and mental health conditions. For example, the prestigious Cleveland Clinic's Center for Integrative Medicine in Ohio offers services—including herbal therapy—to help address the physical, emotional, and spiritual needs of its patients. Other health-care systems such as California-based Kaiser Permanente hospitals and Minnesota-based Mayo Clinic also offer integrative care programs. Medical providers stress that such treatments can be effective if they are added to—and not used as replacements for—conventional medical care.

While herbal products are extremely popular, consumer confidence in their safety is declining because of publicized reports of supplement contamination and manufacturing problems. For example, in 2013 the FDA found that 70 percent of the nation's supplement companies put consumers at risk through dirty equipment that transferred bacteria to vitamins and pesticides to herbal products. These problems are driving the demand for more research and testing of both new and established herbal products.

For example, the University of California, San Francisco Medical Center suggests changes to the regulation of herbal products to improve their safety, including the following:

- Mandating safety tests similar to those required for over-the-counter drugs
- Requiring health claims to be supported by data approved by the FDA
- Ensuring that product labels provide an accurate list of all ingredients

Dr. Murray Feingold of Boston Children's Hospital says, "There is evidence that herbal supplements can be useful in the treatment of certain medical conditions. . . . However, they need to meet the same standards that prescription medications must undergo to prove their effectiveness and safety."

DO IT RIGHT: AVOID THESE HERBAL SUPPLEMENTS

Consumer Reports, a respected and well-known nonprofit magazine that tests and reports on many services and products, compiled a list of herbal supplements to avoid. These nine supplements have been linked to serious side effects and death and can interact with prescription medications. Sufficient evidence to rate their effectiveness does not yet exist.

NAME	USED FOR	POSSIBLE DANGERS
Aconite	Inflammation, joint pain, wounds	Nausea, vomiting, low blood pressure, heart and breathing problems, death
Bitter orange	Weight loss, nasal congestion, allergies	Fainting, heart attack, stroke, death
Chaparral	Weight loss, colds, cancer, infection	Liver and kidney damage
Coltsfoot	Cough, sore throat, bronchitis, asthma	Liver damage, cancer
Comfrey	Heavy menstrual periods, chest pain	Liver damage, cancer
Country mallow	Weight loss, asthma, allergies, bronchitis	Heart attack, stroke, death
Kava or kava-kava	Anxiety	Liver damage
Lobelia	Smoking cessation, coughing	Fast heart rate, very low blood pressure, asthma, bronchitis, coma, possibly death
Yohimbe	Chest pain, depression, diabetes	High or low blood pressure, rapid heart rate, complications, erectile dysfunction, heart problems, death

CHAPTER FIVE

WEIGHT-LOSS SUPPLEMENTS

THERE ARE QUICK WAYS TO LOSE WEIGHT, AND THERE ARE SAFE WAYS TO LOSE WEIGHT. HOWEVER, THERE ARE NO WAYS TO LOSE WEIGHT THAT ARE BOTH QUICK AND SAFE. SUCCESS IN LONG-TERM WEIGHT LOSS REQUIRES PATIENCE, PERSISTENCE, AND HARD WORK TO IMPROVE FOOD CHOICES AND EXERCISE HABITS.
—DIANA WRIGHT, REGISTERED DIETITIAN AND NUTRITION EDUCATOR, 2014

WHEN SEVENTEEN-YEAR-OLD CHRISTOPHER HERRERA OF KATY, TEXAS, WENT TO THE EMERGENCY ROOM, HIS SKIN AND THE WHITES OF HIS EYES WERE BRIGHT YELLOW—ALMOST AS BRIGHT AS A YELLOW HIGHLIGHTER. Doctors soon discovered that Christopher, hoping to lose weight, had taken a concentrated green tea extract, which led to severe liver damage. The damage was so bad that doctors put Christopher on the waiting list for a liver transplant. "It was terrifying," Christopher said. "They kept telling me they had the best surgeons, and they were trying to comfort me. But they were saying that I needed a new liver and that my body could reject it." Doctors saved Christopher's liver, and he did not need a transplant. But because the dietary supplement permanently damaged Christopher's liver, he can no longer play sports, spend much time outdoors, or exert himself physically for fear that he could strain the organ. And he must see a liver specialist every month to monitor the health of his liver.

Doctors know that some FDA-approved medications used to treat cancer, diabetes, and heart disease can damage the liver. Yet when dealing with serious illnesses such as these, doctors weigh the benefit the drugs can provide against the potential for serious side effects. Even acetaminophen, a common over-the-counter pain reliever, may harm the liver if taken in excess. So read labels carefully and follow a doctor's recommendations, even when taking prescription medications.

THE DRIVE TO DIET

Herbal and dietary supplements such as the one Christopher tried are the second most common cause of drug-related liver injuries. Many of the liver-damaging supplements are products that promise people like Christopher that they will lose weight. And Christopher is not alone. At any given time, about one-third of men and one-half of women in the United States are trying to lose weight. By one estimate, Americans spend nearly $2.7 billion per year on meal replacements and diet pills. These products are readily available and convenient to use. And some may work for short periods of time. Just one-third of the Americans who are working to lose weight rely on the only

Most people can get all the nutrients they need from a healthy diet. So-called diet pills can never match the combination of a good exercise program and a healthy diet for weight loss.

scientifically proven method to lose weight successfully: eating less and exercising more.

"Weight loss is tough, and maintaining weight loss is even more difficult," says Diana Wright, a registered dietitian and wellness provider. "Thus any program that offers a quick, easy solution to this challenging problem is appealing. Unfortunately, it is also wishful thinking."

It's hard to lose weight. Eating less food is no picnic. And exercising more often is not a walk in the park. Many people think, why not give that promising natural product a try? People who are worried about their weight may be vulnerable to promises of quick fixes. And like Christopher, they may not understand or they may ignore the potential risks of weight-loss supplements.

WEIGHT-LOSS SUPPLEMENTS IN THE NEWS

Many weight-loss products come from plants. These are some of the most commonly used:

- *Acai berries (right)* are small fruits from the acai palm tree, native to Central and South America. Like all berries, acai berries are high in antioxidants, substances that may prevent or delay cell damage that can lead to cancer and heart disease. Common weight- 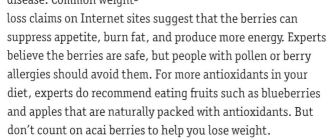 loss claims on Internet sites suggest that the berries can suppress appetite, burn fat, and produce more energy. Experts believe the berries are safe, but people with pollen or berry allergies should avoid them. For more antioxidants in your diet, experts do recommend eating fruits such as blueberries and apples that are naturally packed with antioxidants. But don't count on acai berries to help you lose weight.

- *Apple cider vinegar* is used for killing head lice, cleaning residue from coffeepots, and more. Some people claim that drinking apple cider vinegar can also curb appetite and burn fat, leading to weight loss. Some Internet sites even claim

CLINICAL STUDIES

A clinical study involves research to discover how new medications work in human volunteers. A principal investigator, often a medical doctor, leads the study. Clinical studies also have a research team that includes doctors, nurses, social workers, and other health-care professionals. New prescription medications go through clinical trials, the most rigorous type of study, before they are sold to the public. These are the phases of a clinical trial:

- *Phase 1:* Is the treatment safe? The drug is given for the first time to a small number of healthy volunteers to determine its safety, dosage, and side effects.
- *Phase 2:* Does the treatment work? The drug is given to a larger group of people to determine if it is both safe and effective for the condition it is intended to treat.
- *Phase 3:* How does this treatment compare with existing treatments? This phase involves thousands of people taking the drug at multiple medical centers. It confirms the effectiveness of a drug, monitors side effects, and compares it with other medications used to treat the same condition. These studies are randomized and double-blinded, which means that neither the patient nor the researcher knows if a patient is receiving the real medication or a placebo.
- *Phase 4:* Are there other potential uses for this treatment, and what are the long-term adverse effects? This phase may involve millions of people taking the drug for long periods of time to identify any long-term side effects. During this phase, doctors are legally allowed to use the medication for other purposes than the one for which it was originally intended.

it enhances energy and vitality. A very small study of twelve people found those who ate a piece of bread and drank vinegar felt fuller and, therefore, may have eaten less. However, little scientific evidence supports drinking apple cider vinegar for weight loss.

- *Caffeine*, found naturally in coffee, tea, and chocolate *(below)*—and often added to colas and energy drinks—is a central nervous system stimulant. High-caffeine energy drinks and other stimulants may slightly boost weight loss or prevent weight gain. But they can be dangerous if consumed in excess. Caffeinated drinks, consumed in large doses, have caused seizures, heart problems, high blood pressure, and even death. Manufacturers also sometimes add stimulants, such as ginseng and gingko, to energy drinks. This increases the potential for stimulant-related side effects. Although online claims may suggest that caffeine and other stimulants burn sugar and fat or slow the release of sugar in the bloodstream, doctors don't recommend it for losing weight. Experts say that caffeine may reduce appetite briefly, but it's not proven to aid in long-term weight loss.

- *Capsaicin* is the natural compound that makes hot peppers such as habaneros and jalapeños hot. (It is not found in sweet bell peppers.) Its effect can be similar to caffeine, and online claims often suggest that capsaicin can increase metabolism and burn a lot of calories during exercise. Experts say that capsaicin may slightly curb appetite, which may help with limited weight loss. One study showed obese people on a low-calorie diet who took a synthetic version of capsaicin burned an insignificant 80 calories more a day than those not taking it. Experts view capsaicin as safe, although it may burn the mouth or stomach of people who are not used to it. The key to losing weight long term is reducing calories and increasing daily exercise.

- *Chitosan* is a naturally occurring fiber that is extracted from the shells of crustaceans such as shrimp and crabs. Internet claims suggest that chitosan attracts fats, absorbs water, and excretes them both from the body. However, scientific research does not support chitosan's effectiveness for weight loss. A review of

- high-quality studies shows that taking chitosan tablets for six months may lead to an insignificant weight loss of 1.1 pounds (0.5 kg). Chitosan may be unsafe for people with allergies to shellfish, and it may cause constipation or gas.
- *Conjugated linoleic acid* (CLA) is one of a group of chemicals found in the fatty acid linoleic acid. Dairy products and beef are the major dietary sources of CLA. Online claims for this chemical promise it will help you feel strong and healthy even while dieting. Experts say that studies on humans suggest CLA may help decrease body fat, but it does not seem to decrease body weight. It is generally safe but may cause stomach upset, diarrhea, nausea, and fatigue. Diabetics should not take it without their doctor's approval.
- *Garcinia (below)*, also called hydroxycitric acid, or HCA, comes from a small pumpkin-shaped fruit grown in India, Asia, and Africa. People in those regions say garcinia blocks the appetite. Internet claims promise that taking garcinia diet pills will decrease belly fat, act as a fat blocker, and help stress eaters by balancing mood swings. Experts say that garcinia may help people feel fuller temporarily so they will eat less. Studies on small numbers of people suggest that garcinia may reduce body weight, but clinical trials, which involve much larger numbers of people, have not found the same outcome. Any weight loss from taking garcinia appears to be short term. Side effects are rare, though garcinia may cause nausea or headaches. People with diabetes or Alzheimer's disease should not take garcinia.
- *Glucomannan*, made from the roots of the Asian konjac plant, is a dietary fiber taken to absorb water in the intestines. Some people who take it may feel full and tend to eat less. Internet claims promise the pills will help with appetite control and healthy weight management. Experts say that

only two small controlled studies of twenty and twenty-eight people, respectively, showed a significant weight loss with glucomannan. However, a third similar study of sixty obese children did not show any weight loss. Overall, there is not sufficient evidence to support that glucomannan causes weight loss. It appears safe for most people when taken as a powder or a capsule. However, taking tablets of glucomannan may block the throat or intestines because the tablets may absorb water before fully dissolving.

- *Green tea extract* contains concentrated amounts of the antioxidant catechin. Catechins are in vegetable products, especially in the leaves of green tea plants *(below)*. Various online ads claim that green tea extract supports heart health, healthy aging, and healthy weight. Experts say that catechins *may* decrease appetite, increase fat metabolism, and aid in weight loss, but there is not enough scientific evidence to prove those claims. A study published in 2014 found that green tea extract is the most common dietary supplement associated with liver failure. The average cup of green tea has between 50 to 150 milligrams (0.002 to 0.005 ounces) of catechins. However, some green tea extract pills used for weight loss have more than 700 milligrams (0.02 ounces) of catechins and people often take them several times a day. It is uncertain how many milligrams of catechins are safe. An older study showed that thirty-eight people who drank 690 milligrams (0.02 ounces) of catechins as tea for twelve weeks had no side effects. Play it safe. Talk to your doctor first. And if you decide to try green tea extract for weight loss, limit it to no more than three to four cups a day.

- *Hoodia* is made from a South African succulent plant long used as an appetite suppressant by indigenous peoples. Online sites promoting the diet pills claim they will suppress appetite and stimulate a positive mood. Some studies suggest hoodia may suppress appetite. One study of seven people showed they lost, on average, 3.3 percent of their body weight. Such a small study has little or no scientific merit, however. In another study, hoodia caused vomiting, odd skin sensations, and increased blood pressure and heart rate. Experts at the Mayo Clinic and at the Cedars-Sinai Medical Center in Los Angeles do not recommend hoodia for weight loss.

- *Human chorionic gonadotropin* (HCG) is a hormone that women produce naturally during pregnancy. Doctors use it legally to treat infertility and other medical conditions. Although the FDA views the use of HCG for weight loss as illegal, the hormone is still widely available in drinkable and injectable forms. Supporters claim that using HCG leads to significant weight loss of up to 1 pound (0.5 kg) a day. But to be successful at losing weight, people taking HCG must also stick to an extremely strict and unhealthy diet of 500 to 800 calories a day. "It's reckless, irresponsible, and completely irrational," says Dr. Pieter Cohen, assistant professor of medicine at Harvard Medical School. "Can you lose weight on (HCG)? Of course, but that's because you're hardly consuming any calories." Experts say teen girls need at least 1,600 calories a day while dieting, and teen boys need at least 2,000. Even so, shady weight-loss clinics still offer the product. Side effects include headache, blood clots, leg cramps, hair loss, constipation, and breast tenderness.

- *Raspberry ketone* is a natural chemical extracted from red raspberries *(below)*. Supplement manufacturers sell raspberry ketone pills for weight loss. Online promotions for the diet pills claim they increase metabolism, reduce body fat, and generally support healthy living. One article about a small study of forty-five obese people—who followed a reduced calorie diet, exercised, and took a raspberry ketone supplement—showed that the participants "lost more fat mass and waist girth." Yet the same article also noted that "adherence to the weight loss program led to beneficial changes in body fat in placebo [a fake pill]." So the key to weight loss in this study was to stick to the diet and exercise program. It didn't matter very much whether the subjects took the diet pill. Raspberry ketones are believed to stimulate the release of norepinephrine, a stress hormone normally produced by the body. The hormone, among other functions, increases heart rate and blood pressure. For this reason, raspberry ketone pills may be dangerous for people with asthma, emphysema, and high blood pressure.

PULLED FROM THE SHELVES

While the FDA is not authorized to approve dietary supplements before they become available for sale, the agency can take action when health-care providers or consumers report harmful effects from a supplement. The FDA can also take action if a supplement manufacturer fails to seek approval for an ingredient not in use before 1994.

Ma huang (also called ephedra) is an herbal supplement the FDA banned because of dangerous side effects. Ephedra contains

DO IT RIGHT: HERE'S WHAT IT TAKES

The National Weight Control Registry is the largest ongoing research project in the United States investigating how people succeed at losing weight and keeping it off. The registry tracks more than ten thousand Americans who have lost at least 30 pounds (14 kg) and kept it off for one year or more. Registry members report a few key actions linked to their success:

- More than half of those who lost weight enrolled in a reputable weight-loss program. Nearly all modified their food intake, including cutting down on high-calorie foods and eating more vegetables and fruits.
- Most exercise about one hour a day, with walking the most common exercise.
- Most eat breakfast every day.
- About three-fourths weigh themselves weekly.
- About two-thirds watch fewer than ten hours of television a week.

Ephedra sinensis *is known as ma huang in Chinese medicine. The plant contains ephedrine and pseudoephedrine. Once used in weight-loss and sports supplements, the FDA banned it in 2004 because of serious side effects.*

the stimulant ephedrine, similar to amphetamine (speed), and pseudoephedrine, a related chemical. Ma huang has been used as part of Chinese folk medicine for centuries to treat asthma, headaches, flu, and nasal congestion. In the 1990s, many Americans used ephedra in weight-loss and sports supplements. Hundreds of dangerous reactions were reported among those who took it, including high blood pressure, heart attacks, strokes, seizures, and even death.

In 2004 the FDA banned the sale of dietary supplements containing ephedra in the United States. At the time, consumers were purchasing about $100 million of ephedra products each year. Despite numerous appeals by supplement manufacturers to reverse the ban, US courts upheld the FDA's ban.

The FDA also took action against aegeline, a chemical found in the bael tree of India and Southeast Asia. People in these regions of the world have long used parts of the bael tree for food and medicine. However, bael had not been used in the United States before 1994. For that reason, under the DSHEA law, aegeline products are among those that should have received FDA approval before manufacturers could legally sell products containing the chemical.

A company selling a popular weight-loss supplement that contained aegeline had added the ingredient early in 2013 to replace the controversial stimulant 1,3-dimethylamylamine (DMAA), which the FDA had declared illegal. However, the company had not sought FDA approval for aegeline. Later in 2013, while investigating reported cases of liver failure possibly related to the supplement, the FDA discovered aegeline was in the product.

The FDA wrote a letter to the company, pointing out that the FDA had no information to show that aegeline had been marketed in the United States prior to the 1994 cutoff date established by DSHEA. In response, the company claimed that because aegeline comes from a tree that has been in existence for centuries, it did not view the chemical as a new product requiring FDA approval.

While the debate over aegeline continued, reports of dozens of people in Hawaii who suffered sudden and severe liver disease reached the FDA. Reports about patients with liver failure in other states soon began surfacing as well. Of these patients, 83 percent had used

LISTEN TO YOUR GUT

Does a weight-loss supplement you are considering make any of these claims?

1. Lose at least 2 pounds (0.9 kg) a week without dieting or exercise.
2. Lose weight no matter what you eat.
3. Weight loss is permanent even after you stop the supplement.
4. Everyone can lose substantial weight with this supplement.
5. Lose weight by wearing a skin patch or by rubbing a cream into the skin.

According to the US Federal Trade Commission, claims such as these are scams. The only scientifically proven way to lose weight and to keep it off is through healthy eating and regular exercise. If you are considering taking a weight-loss supplement, check with your health-care provider first.

weight-loss supplements containing aegeline in the weeks before they became ill.

In November 2013, at the urging of the FDA and the Hawaii Department of Health, the supplement company voluntarily recalled and destroyed its aegeline-based products. Even so, the company disputed the safety concerns surrounding the supplement. The recall came too late for many people, however. Nearly one hundred people suffered liver failure, three required liver transplants, and one died.

Registered dietitian Diana Wright cautions that "the dangers of taking weight loss supplements include, at the minimum, the high risk of rebound weight gain. And in the worst-case scenario, the use of unproven weight loss supplements has resulted in the death of some users."

CHAPTER SIX

SPORTS SUPPLEMENTS

SPORTS SUPPLEMENTS WILL NOT TURN YOU INTO THE NEXT ALL-STAR. SCIENTIFIC EVIDENCE SUGGESTS MANY OF THE SUPPLEMENTS ON THE MARKET ACTUALLY DECREASE ATHLETIC PERFORMANCE. TEEN ATHLETES WOULD BE WISE TO PUT THEIR FAITH IN HARD WORK AND DISCIPLINE RATHER THAN LOOKING FOR A QUICK FIX
—TREVOR GILLUM, PHD, 2014

IN 2011 US ARMY PRIVATE MICHAEL LEE SPARLING DIED AT THE AGE OF TWENTY-TWO. But he didn't die from a roadside bomb or an ambush in Afghanistan. Instead, he collapsed and died of sudden cardiac arrest after a ten-minute run with his unit at Fort Bliss, Texas. Sparling had recently graduated from basic training and was in excellent physical condition.

A few weeks before his death, Sparling had started taking a daily workout supplement containing the powerful stimulant DMAA. Sparling didn't have to go online or to a street dealer to get DMAA. He purchased it legally at a national chain nutrition store on the Fort Bliss base. The supplement, advertised as all natural, promised to boost workout energy and improve stamina.

Health experts say the side effects of DMAA are similar to those of amphetamine and include chest pain, breathing difficulties, and seizures. The military soon linked the deaths of two other young soldiers at Fort Bliss to DMAA. As a result of the deaths, the US

Department of Defense (DOD) studied two thousand active-duty military personnel and discovered more than 15 percent were taking DMAA. Forty of the soldiers told a military doctor they were sick, and two developed liver failure. In December 2011, the DOD removed all products with DMAA from stores on American military bases. US federal marshals seized more than $2 million of the banned product from the manufacturer in November 2013.

WHO TAKES **WHAT?**

The market for sports supplements is huge and is growing at an estimated rate of 24 percent each year. The industry may be worth at least $91 billion worldwide. One survey of American adolescents found that about 1.6 percent of teens—1.2 million of them—take supplements, hoping to improve sports performance.

Approximately 7.7 million US high school students participate in sports. Many teens want to have stronger muscles and to excel in their sports. And many believe sports supplements can help. Sports supplements—also called ergogenic aids—are products to enhance athletic performance and stamina. Manufacturers say these supplements improve strength, increase stamina, and hasten workout recovery time.

Exercise and a good diet are a safe way to build strength and speed.

Researchers have studied the use of some sports supplements among children and teens. One study published in 2012 looked at the medical records of more than ninety-four hundred people under the age of eighteen. The study asked if the participants had taken a vitamin or mineral supplement or an herb hoping to enhance sports performance. Of those who said they had, most had taken multivitamins, minerals, or both. Others took fiber, fish oil, or fatty acids. More than one-third took the amino acid creatine to build muscle mass. Twice as many boys as girls reported using supplements to improve their sports performance. (The study did not ask whether the supplements had actually improved athletic performance.)

In another 2012 study, researchers asked twenty-eight hundred teen athletes what they had done to increase their muscle size or tone over the past year. The most common responses were exercising more often and eating better. About one-third of the respondents also used protein powders or shakes. One out of ten teens reported using products such as creatine and other amino acids, dehydroepiandrosterone (DHEA), or growth hormone. Nearly 6 percent reported taking steroids, with nearly three times as many boys as girls using steroids. (The study did not ask whether the supplements had actually improved athletic performance.)

Trevor Gillum, an associate professor of kinesiology, is an exercise physiologist (a person who studies the science of exercise) at California Baptist University in Riverside, California. He doesn't believe teen

> **The reality is that gains in [athletic] performance are realized through hard work, proper nutrition, and adequate rest.**
>
> —Trevor Gillum, associate professor of kinesiology at California Baptist University in Riverside, California

athletes need sports supplements. "Most athletes are looking for a 'magic bullet,' though they may not admit that to others. The chance of any dietary supplement improving performance in high school athletes is slim. Empirical data suggests that most supplements do not increase performance. So while athletes take them in hopes of leapfrogging the competition, the reality is that gains in performance are realized through hard work, proper nutrition, and adequate rest."

SPORTS SUPPLEMENTS IN THE NEWS

Sports supplements come in pills and tablets, powders and creams, and liquids taken by mouth or injected with needles. Three commonly used categories of sports supplements include amino acids, steroids, and stimulants. Some are legal, and others are not.

AMINO ACIDS

The body uses these chemicals to build proteins. Our body can make all but nine of the amino acids we need. These nine are called the essential amino acids. We must obtain them from foods. The essential amino acids occur naturally in foods that contain protein, such as meat, poultry, fish, and eggs. When people eat these foods, the body breaks down the animal proteins and turns them into human proteins. Many athletes take extra protein in the form of tablets, protein powders, and sports bars, believing they will enhance sports performance by increasing muscle mass and strength. However, eating extra protein does little to build muscle or strength. Eating too much protein may damage the kidneys. People should not skip carbs in favor of protein, or overall health can suffer.

Branched-chain amino acids (leucine, isoleucine, and valine) are three of the essential amino acids the body cannot make. *Branched-chain* refers to the chemical structure of these amino acids. Like all amino acids, they are found in foods that contain protein. Doctors use these amino acids to treat certain medical conditions, such as brain and movement disorders. Athletes use branched-chain amino acids in pill form to improve exercise performance and to reduce muscle breakdown during exercise.

WebMD, an accredited source of health information with a popular website of the same name, says branched-chain amino acids are possibly effective for reducing muscle breakdown during exercise but may be ineffective at improving overall athletic performance. They appear to be safe for most people when used for six months or less. Side effects are rare but include fatigue and loss of coordination. They may interact with some prescription medications.

Creatine is one of the most widely marketed legal dietary supplements. It is an amino acid normally found in the body that the liver, kidneys, and pancreas produce naturally. It also occurs in meat and fish. The body stores most of its creatine in muscles. Once muscles have all the creatine they can hold, the kidneys excrete the excess. So unless a person's body is deficient in creatine—which can occur with a relatively rare genetic condition—such supplements will have little or no impact on athletic performance.

Creatine does benefit some adult athletes for the first few minutes of high-intensity exercise such as sprinting and weight lifting. However, it does not appear to benefit endurance or aerobic activities. Studies on creatine use among adults find that it is likely safe for completely healthy adults who are on no other medications or stimulants (including caffeinated beverages). However, teens make

Fish and meat are a good source of amino acids and creatine for teens.

up a large portion of creatine users, and its impact on teens has not been adequately studied. For this reason, the American College of Sports Medicine recommends that people under the age of eighteen should not take creatine. Among many known side effects are weight gain, dehydration, muscle cramps, asthma-like symptoms, high blood pressure, confusion, and kidney failure.

"Get protein, amino acids, and creatine from foods purchased at the grocery store," says Gillum. "These are all part of an appropriate diet. What's more, teen athletes will spend far more money purchasing these supplements than if they ate a balanced diet."

Anabolic Steroids

Correctly called anabolic-androgenic steroids (AAS), these manufactured chemicals are similar to testosterone, a hormone that males naturally produce to regulate and maintain physical and sexual development. AAS, along with stimulants, are among the chemicals known as performance-enhancing drugs (PEDs). AAS include many substances that are either chemically related to testosterone or that the body will change into a testosterone-like chemical. AAS supplements come in many forms, including pills, creams, and injectable liquid.

Some athletes take AAS supplements for the anabolic effect. When used with a good training program and a healthy diet, AAS supplements increase muscle mass and strength. AAS also have an androgenic effect. They enhance secondary male sexual characteristics. For example, AAS can deepen the voice and enlarge the Adam's apple. They increase acne and body hair. Bones become heavier. The chest and shoulders broaden.

Known side effects of AAS steroids include the following:
- Liver and kidney damage
- High blood pressure, high cholesterol, and heart disease
- Shrinking of the testicles, impotence, and sterility
- Breast enlargement in males
- Decreased height, if taken before growth is complete
- Psychological problems such as depression, insomnia, and increased aggressive or violent behavior (roid rage)
- Development of male traits in females (facial hair, a deep voice)

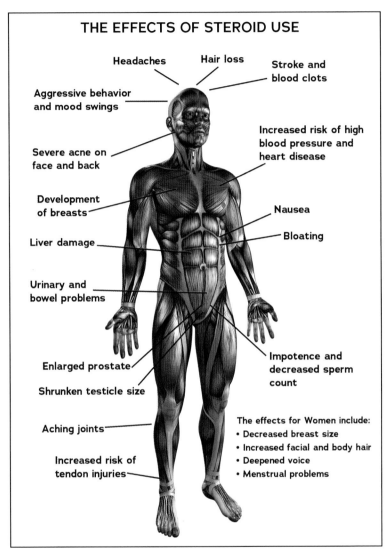

THE EFFECTS OF STEROID USE

Headaches

Hair loss

Stroke and blood clots

Aggressive behavior and mood swings

Increased risk of high blood pressure and heart disease

Severe acne on face and back

Development of breasts

Nausea

Bloating

Liver damage

Urinary and bowel problems

Enlarged prostate

Shrunken testicle size

Impotence and decreased sperm count

Aching joints

Increased risk of tendon injuries

The effects for Women include:
• Decreased breast size
• Increased facial and body hair
• Deepened voice
• Menstrual problems

In the United States, AAS steroids are illegal without a prescription. Doctors may use AAS to treat specific medical conditions such as delayed puberty, cancer, muscular dystrophy, and breast cancer in women. The FDA does not consider AAS to be a form of dietary supplements. The agency considers them to be in a category of new drugs that have not been approved in clinical studies.

Supplements containing illegal steroids are often sold anyway, often through reputable online sites that sell supplements. Sometimes the FDA discovers the illegal substance through random testing of new supplements. For example, in December 2013, the FDA warned consumers to stop using a popular product marketed as a dietary supplement for muscle growth. The label showed the supplement contained a chemical called 18-Methylestr-4-en-3-one-17b-ol, which the FDA determined to be a synthetic AAS. Experts believe the supplement caused liver failure in a formerly healthy twenty-eight-year-old man who had taken it for several weeks. The man became critically ill and required a lifesaving liver transplant.

With a staggering number of illegal AAS available online and elsewhere, consumers should be highly suspicious of any product claiming it can build muscle or lean body mass. AAS products have complex chemical names, and consumers may not realize these ingredients are actually forms of illegal AAS. Watch out for steroidal chemicals such as these:

- 19-Norandrosta-4,9-diene-3,17 dione
- 17a-methyl-etioallocholan-2-ene-17b-ol
- 19-norandrostenedione
- 2,17a-dimethyl-5a-androsta-1-en-17b-ol-3-one
- Androstenedione
- Methylnortestosterone acetate

Stimulants

Like AAS, stimulants hide behind an indecipherable alphabet soup, making it hard for consumers to know what's really inside the product. The DMAA that led to Private Michael Lee Sparling's death is one such stimulant. N,alpha-diethylphenylethylamine (N,a-DEPEA) is another illegal supplement, which researchers have found to be similar to methamphetamine, a dangerous street drug. N,a-DEPEA is less potent than methamphetamine but more potent than ephedra, a stimulant the FDA banned in 2004 after research linked that drug to heart attacks and death. Amphetamine- and methamphetamine-like chemicals speed up the body's nervous system.

Dr. Pieter Cohen of Harvard Medical School cautions, "Alarmingly, we have found [N,a-DEPEA, a stimulant] in a mainstream sports supplement that has never been studied in humans. The health risk of using supplements adulterated with a drug should not be underestimated." Dr. Victor Navarro of Philadelphia's Einstein Healthcare Network adds, "You have to assume that all supplements have potential to cause injury."

Dietitian and sports nutrition counselor Nancy Clark reminds young athletes that "no supplement can compensate for lousy eating. Nor can you out-train a poor sports diet. The best bet is to meet with a registered dietitian who is also a sports dietitian to create a personalized food plan that works for you and your lifestyle."

BANNED FROM COMPETITION

Doping refers to the use of banned performance-enhancing drugs, such as AAS, among athletes. Some organizations carry responsibility for ensuring that athletes do not use AAS or any other PED. For example, the National Federation of State High School Associations (NFHS) educates American high school athletes about sports medicine, sporting activities, and concussion. It strongly discourages the use of PEDs by high school athletes. The National Collegiate Athletic Association (NCAA) is committed to enforcing the rules and creating fair competition for student athletes enrolled in American colleges and universities. As part of this mission, the NCAA assists member colleges in collecting and testing thousands of blood and urine samples from athletes each year. It also maintains a list of banned drugs that includes stimulants, anabolic steroids, and street drugs. An athlete who tests positive for the first time for a street drug or a PED faces a full one-year suspension. A second positive test for a PED leads to permanent suspension from collegiate sports.

All professional sports organizations, such as the National Football League and Major League Baseball, promote fair play and monitor athletes for illegal drug use. Professional athletes are likely to suffer large monetary losses when they are suspended, whether it is for a single game or an entire season.

The U.S. Anti-Doping Agency (USADA) is the organization responsible for ensuring that American athletes who participate in the Olympics and other international sporting events leading up to the Games do not take illegal PEDs. The International Olympic Committee

NATIONAL FEDERATION OF STATE HIGH SCHOOL ASSOCIATIONS

The National Federation of State High School Associations has led the development of sporting activities in American high schools since 1920. It establishes standards and rules for competition, among other functions. In 2012 the Sports Medicine Advisory Committee of the NFHS published its official position statement on the use of AAS by high school athletes. The statement reads:

The NFHS strongly opposes the use of anabolic, androgenic steroids and other performance-enhancing substances by high school athletes. Such use violates legal, ethical, and competitive equity standards, and imposes unacceptable long-term health risks. The NFHS supports prohibitions by educational institutions, amateur and professional organizations, and governmental regulators on the use of anabolic steroids and other controlled substances, except as specifically prescribed by physicians for therapeutic purposes. Anabolic, androgenic steroids are prohibited by all sports governing organizations.

(IOC) has a similar focus. For example, at the 2014 Winter Olympics in Sochi, Russia, IOC officials performed nearly twenty-five hundred urine and blood tests among competing athletes. These tests included pre-competition testing, random testing, and testing of the top five winners in all events. The IOC keeps samples for eight years for retroactive testing in the event that improved technology becomes available or if an athlete is later suspected of doping.

Some of the substances banned for Olympic athletes include stimulants such as ephedra or ephedra-like products, at least twenty-five AAS, HCG, narcotics, cannabis, diuretics (medications that increase urine production and that can mask the presence of other drugs), and certain prescription medications that can enhance athletic performance even when used legally (glucocorticoids and beta-blockers among others). Athletes found to be using these banned substances will be disqualified from competition, even if the athlete didn't know that a particular product contained a banned substance.

DOPING IN THE NEWS

Some of the biggest, most powerful names in sports—Tyson Gay, Lance Armstrong, and Alex Rodriguez, among others—have been caught doping. In July 2013, US sprinter and Olympian Tyson Gay held the fastest time for the 100-meter dash. He was ready to challenge world record holder Usain Bolt at the 2013 World Championships to be held in Moscow the next month. But Gay failed his mandatory pre-competition USADA drug test and was not allowed to compete in Moscow. Gay had used a sports cream that listed testosterone and DHEA among its ingredients. DHEA is a hormone the body converts to testosterone. The label also listed somatotropin—human growth hormone—on its label. All three substances are banned by the USADA and by the IOC for Olympic athletes.

During a press conference, Gay told reporters, "I don't have a sabotage story. I don't have any lies. I don't have anything to say to make this seem like it was a mistake or it was on U.S. Anti-Doping Agency's hands. . . . I basically put my trust in someone [a chiropractor specializing in antiaging medicine] and I was let down." According to Gay, the label on the jar stated the ingredients were 100 percent natural. The chiropractor had also told him that football players had used the cream and passed drug tests.

In 2014 the USADA temporarily suspended sprinter Tyson Gay from competition for use of banned substances.

The next year, in May, the USADA announced a one-year suspension of Gay based on his drug-testing results. Normally, a ban for doping is two years, but Gay's suspension was reduced because he cooperated with the agency to provide information about others potentially involved in doping. As part of his penalty, Gay also accepted disqualification of results dating back to July 15, 2012, the date when he first used a product that contained a banned substance. That year he had been a member of the Silver Medal relay team at the London Olympics. Gay was forced to return his medal to the US Olympic Committee.

In 2012, based on volumes of testimony and other evidence proving that superstar cyclist Lance Armstrong had used illegal PEDs, the USADA banned him from cycling competition for life and stripped him of his seven Tour de France titles. He was also expected to repay millions of dollars to the US Postal Service, which had sponsored Armstrong and his team. Armstrong had for years vehemently denied using these drugs. However, in January 2013—in the face of irrefutable evidence including sworn testimony from former teammates—he admitted that he had, in fact, used PEDs throughout his cycling career. He admitted to receiving banned blood transfusions and testosterone.

Bicyclist Lance Armstrong, seven-time winner of the Tour de France. The USADA pulled Armstrong's medals after he admitted to years of steroid use and blood doping.

BLOOD DOPING

Some athletes use blood doping to improve their performance. Blood doping increases the number of red blood cells in the body. Because red blood cells carry oxygen, the athlete who undergoes blood doping may have more stamina, especially in long-distance events such as running and cycling. The USADA, the IOC, and other legitimate sports organizations ban blood doping. Blood tests can identify if athletes are guilty of blood doping.

The three commonly used forms of blood doping are the following:

- **Blood transfusions.** Athletes may have their own blood drawn and stored. The athletes then transfuse their own stored blood prior to the athletic event. Red blood cells in the stored blood, when added to those already in the bloodstream, give the athlete a higher-than-normal number of oxygen-carrying red blood cells. More oxygen in the body often means better athletic performance. However, having too many red blood cells thickens the blood and increases the risk for blood clots and stroke. Medically, doctors use blood transfusions legitimately during surgery or when a patient has lost blood due to illness or injury.

- **Erythropoietin (EPO)** is an injectable hormone that stimulates the production of red blood cells and can improve athletic performance. Doctors may legally give EPO to patients with anemia, kidney failure, or cancer to increase the number of red blood cells. It is illegal in sporting competition.

- **Synthetic oxygen carriers.** These manufactured chemicals carry a limited amount of oxygen and are injected directly into the bloodstream. They are used for the emergency care of patients who are bleeding, when human blood is not available, or there is not enough time to match the blood type. They are illegal in athletic competition.

He also said he'd taken erythropoietin, a substance that stimulates the body to form more oxygen-carrying red blood cells. Used in this illegal manner, the process is called blood doping. "I view this situation as one big lie that I repeated a lot of times," Armstrong said during an interview with TV personality Oprah Winfrey. "The truth isn't what I said. I'm a flawed character, as I well know."

In 2007 baseball phenomenon Alex Rodriguez signed a ten-year, $275 million contract with the New York Yankees. That year another

Major League Baseball suspended Alex Rodriguez for the entire 2014 season after evidence surfaced that linked him to the use of performance-enhancing drugs.

ballplayer accused Rodriguez of using PEDs. By 2009 rumors were circulating in the sports world that Rodriguez had used PEDs for years. He vehemently denied the charges. Major League Baseball (MLB) officials suspended him in 2013 after the man who ran a Florida antiaging clinic testified that he personally had injected Rodriguez with illegal PEDs. He also turned over incriminating e-mails that showed Rodriguez had asked for PEDs. Rodriguez's suspension for 211 games was the harshest penalty in MLB history.

After months of appeal and arbitration, the MLB reduced Rodriguez's suspension to 162 games—the entire 2014 season. MLB commissioner Bud Selig said Rodriguez will have a clean slate at the end of his suspension. "A guy does something, he gets disciplined, he comes back. We shouldn't keep penalizing him." Rodriguez admits to injecting something but says he didn't know exactly what he was injecting. "I knew we weren't taking Tic Tacs."

WORTH THE RISK?

Athletes who use illegal PEDs gamble their careers and professional reputations to achieve a competitive edge. They do so, in part, because the financial gains associated with winning can be extremely lucrative. A football player who is part of a winning Super Bowl team wins a $92,000 bonus (on top of a multimillion-dollar salary). The Tour de France winner receives more than $500,000. And an Olympic gold medal winner receives $25,000. But when an athlete is caught, the penalties are heavy. For example, Alex Rodriguez lost an estimated $25 million in salary for the 2014 season.

Athletes who take illegal PEDs risk not only their financial livelihood and their reputations but their health as well. And it is not unusual for athletes found guilty of doping to say they do not know exactly what they took. Sometimes this is true. Unscrupulous coaches or trainers sometimes provide the drugs without explaining what they are. Each athlete must decide if it is worth the risk to take PEDs or any other unknown substance. Amy Eichner, special adviser on Drug Reference and Supplement Strategy for the USADA, says, "No consumer can ever know what's inside a bottle. We advise our athletes that all supplement use is at their own risk."

DO IT RIGHT: HANDLING PRESSURE AND COMPETITION

Many ads for sports supplements are aimed at teens. Ads may show dramatic before-and-after pictures that make it look easy to get a great body from a pill or powder quickly. Like adult athletes, teen athletes are under a lot of pressure to look better and to excel in sports. TeensHealth (at http://www.teenshealth.org) is part of the Nemours Foundation based in Jacksonville, Florida. This prestigious organization provides accurate health information endorsed by doctors to teens around the clock. It offers these suggestions for dealing with pressure:

- Make downtime a priority. Teens need more than eight hours of sleep each night.
- Learn to relax. Take a few minutes to meditate and visualize yourself succeeding at sports activities.
- Say no to harmful substances.
- Train smarter. Work on improving cardiovascular conditioning as well as muscle groups.
- Always check with your doctor before taking any sports supplement.

CHAPTER SEVEN

BUYER BEWARE

> HEALTH FRAUD IS A PERVASIVE PROBLEM, ESPECIALLY WHEN SCAMMERS SELL ONLINE. IT'S DIFFICULT TO TRACK DOWN THE RESPONSIBLE PARTIES. WHEN WE DO FIND THEM AND TELL THEM THEIR PRODUCTS ARE ILLEGAL, SOME WILL SHUT DOWN THEIR WEBSITE. UNFORTUNATELY, HOWEVER, THESE SAME PRODUCTS MAY REAPPEAR LATER ON A DIFFERENT WEBSITE, AND SOMETIMES MAY REAPPEAR WITH A DIFFERENT NAME.
> —GARY COODY, NATIONAL HEALTH FRAUD COORDINATOR, FDA, 2014

FOR NEARLY A YEAR, TERESA CANTWELL, FIFTY-FIVE, OF ROCKVILLE CENTRE, NEW YORK, AND HER TWENTY-SEVEN-YEAR-OLD DAUGHTER TOOK THE MULTI-B VITAMINS THAT HER CHIROPRACTOR HAD RECOMMENDED FOR LOWERING CHOLESTEROL AND FOR ACHIEVING A ROBUST STATE OF HEALTH. Instead, Cantwell's cholesterol rose to an abnormally high level, and her voice and her daughter's became deeper and more masculine. Cantwell also said her daughter's liver enzymes rose and her menstrual periods stopped. Both women are still recovering from the side effects of the vitamins. "We were essentially poisoned," she said.

Teresa Cantwell and her daughter had good reason to believe they were poisoned. The vitamins they took contained multiple illegal anabolic steroids, which explained the elevated cholesterol, cessation of menstrual periods, and deepened voices. And the Cantwells weren't alone in their experience. The tainted supplements sickened nearly thirty people in all and sent one to the hospital.

In 2013 the US Department of Justice filed a lawsuit against the manufacturer of the vitamins. The company admitted to knowingly selling adulterated dietary supplements containing anabolic steroids. In 2014 the company agreed to halt all operations during the federal investigation.

CONTAMINATION!

In the world of dietary supplements, contaminants are substances accidentally or purposefully added to a product at the factory during production or packaging. For example, a piece of equipment may be used to prepare different herbs for supplements without proper cleaning between uses. If that happens, a supplement may contain unintended traces of other ingredients. Contamination may also come from the environment. Human hair and rodent droppings, for instance, can make their way into products during the manufacturing or processing stages. Consumers should be especially wary of dietary supplements imported from other countries. For example, China is a major supplier to the United States of the ingredients used to make supplements, especially those for vitamins A, B, C, D, and E. China has repeatedly been caught exporting contaminated products.

Manufacturers in the United States are legally required to list every ingredient in a dietary supplement on the product label. However, unethical manufacturers may add ingredients and then fail to list them. For example, the maker of a weight-loss supplement may add but not list a diuretic. The diuretic will rid the body of some fluids through urination, resulting in short-term weight loss. However, it also increases thirst. The person who takes the supplement may then drink more fluids to make up for the lost water and is likely to gain back any lost weight.

Whether the contamination occurs by accident or on purpose, tainted products are more common than you might think. For instance, the online peer-reviewed journal *BMC Medicine,* based in the United Kingdom, published a study in 2013 that found serious discrepancies between herbal products inside bottles and the ingredients listed on

Dietary supplements may be contaminated at a factory during production or packaging.

the labels. In that study, scientists tested the DNA of forty-four herbal products sold by twelve different companies in North America. Nearly 60 percent of the products contained DNA from plant species not listed on the labels.

The study's authors concluded that "most of the herbal products tested were of poor quality, including considerable product substitution, contamination, and use of fillers. These activities dilute the effectiveness of otherwise useful remedies, lowering the perceived value of all related products because of a lack of consumer confidence in them."

WATCH OUT FOR THESE CONTAMINANTS

The FDA has funds to run one thousand random tests of dietary supplements each year out of the estimated eight-five thousand supplement products on the market. During two years of random testing, the FDA found hidden drugs or steroids in more than 170 dietary supplements. The supplements contained unexpected ingredients including controlled substances such as narcotics, seizure medications, prescription drugs, and drugs not approved for sale in

> ## I'm convinced that many of the supplements on the market today contain illegal products.
>
> —Trevor Gillum, assistant professor of kinesiology, California Baptist University, Riverside, California

the United States. Unscrupulous manufacturers may add these ingredients to make their products more effective, knowing that it is illegal and dangerous to do so. Trevor Gillum says, "I'm convinced that many of the supplements on the market today contain illegal products. Since the FDA does not regulate the supplement industry, there is no way of knowing how widespread the contamination really is." Contaminants and undeclared ingredients found in dietary supplements for sale in the United States have included the following:

- Walnut residue, which can be deadly to people with nut allergies, has been found in ginkgo- and echinacea-based products.
- A bottle labeled as St. John's wort contained laxative tablets but none of the herb itself.
- Some herbs in herbal products contained amphetamine-like ingredients.
- Dozens of weight-loss supplements contained the prescription drug sibutramine, which the FDA took off the market in 2010 after doctors linked it to heart problems.
- Traces of penicillin were found in dietary supplements. The antibiotic can be deadly to people with penicillin allergies.
- Phenolphthalein was once available as an over-the-counter laxative. The FDA removed it from the market because it was believed to cause cancer. It has been found in weight-loss supplements.
- Bumetanide, a potent prescription diuretic, was found in a weight-loss product. It can cause severe dehydration and low

blood pressure.
- Vitamins and mineral supplements have been found to be contaminated with bacteria and pesticides.
- An over-the-counter supplement marketed for insomnia contained the prescription-only medications doxepin (a sleep medicine) and chlorpromazine (a powerful antipsychotic drug).
- An arthritis supplement contained ibuprofen, an over-the-counter-medication that can be dangerous for some people with asthma. It also may cause stomach pain, heartburn, nausea, vomiting, and constipation in some people.
- A red yeast rice supplement, marketed to lower cholesterol, contained the prescription-only medication lovastatin, a well-known cholesterol-lowering medication.

ARE YOU TOXIC?

Toxins—such as alcohol, drugs, or poisons such as lead and mercury—can lead to a long list of ailments including headaches, bloating, arthritis, fatigue, depression, illness, and even death. Detoxification describes medical treatments used to rid the body of such toxins. Online vendors sell thousands of detoxification products promising to detoxify you and make you feel better. One popular site offers 5,234 supplements and other items promoted as detoxification products. The risks associated with using detox products include dehydration, imbalance of the electrolytes sodium and potassium, loss of important nutrients, and disruption of helpful intestinal bacteria.

Frank Sacks, MD, of the Harvard School of Public Health, says that suggesting that the body needs help detoxifying "has no basis in human biology." Your organs and immune system handle those duties, no matter what you eat. The human body comes fully equipped with an excellent detoxification system made up of the liver, kidneys, lungs, intestines, the skin, and the immune system. So skip the detox supplements and concentrate on giving your body what it needs to maintain its hardy self-cleaning system—a good diet, drinking enough fluids, exercising regularly, and getting enough sleep.

TIP-OFFS TO **RIP-OFFS**

Health fraud has been around for a long time. According to the FDA, health fraud is the deceptive promotion, advertising, distribution, or sale of a product said to prevent, diagnose, treat, cure, or lessen an illness, in the absence of scientific proof.

It would be nice if fraudulent supplements came with flashing red warning signs. But they don't, and scammers are smart about using pop-up ads, spam, and other methods to reach consumers. The FDA suggests that consumers watch for common scams, false claims, and rip-offs such as these:

- *One product does it all.* Be suspicious of products that claim to cure a wide range of diseases. A New York firm claimed its products marketed as dietary supplements could treat or cure senile dementia; brain atrophy; atherosclerosis; kidney dysfunction; gangrene; depression; osteoarthritis; dysuria; and lung, cervical, and prostate cancer. In October 2012, at FDA's request, US marshals seized these products.

- *Personal testimonials.* Success stories, such as, "It cured my diabetes" or "My tumors are gone," are easy to make up and are not a substitute for scientific evidence.

- *Quick fixes.* Few diseases or conditions can be treated quickly, even with legitimate products. Beware of language such as, "Lose 30 pounds [14 kg] in thirty days" or "eliminates skin cancer in days."

- *"All natural."* Some plants found in nature (such as poisonous mushrooms) can kill when consumed. Moreover, FDA has found numerous products promoted as "all natural" but contain hidden and dangerously high doses of prescription drug ingredients or even untested active artificial ingredients.

- *"Miracle cure."* Alarms should go off when you see this claim or others like it such as, "new discovery," "scientific breakthrough," or "secret ingredient." If a real cure for a serious disease were discovered, it would be widely reported through the media and prescribed by health professionals—not buried in print ads, TV infomercials, or on Internet sites.

- *Conspiracy theories*. Claims like "The pharmaceutical industry and the government are working together to hide information about a miracle cure" are always untrue and unfounded. These statements are used to distract consumers from the obvious, common-sense questions about the so-called miracle cure.

THINK TWICE

If you and your health-care provider decide you need a dietary supplement, try to ensure the supplement is as safe as possible. Start by reading the dietary supplement fact sheet about the product from the National Institutes of Health, Office of Dietary Supplements at http://ods.od.nih.gov/factsheets/list-all/. Consider selecting single-ingredient supplements over those with multiple ingredients. That way, if you feel better or worse, you know which ingredient caused the change.

Think about phoning the manufacturer (not the seller) of the supplement you want to take. Tell the customer service agent what kind of information you are seeking and ask to speak to the person who can help you. You might ask what evidence the company has to support its claims and if the company has received complaints about the product. The FDA maintains adverse events reports—filed by health-care providers or individuals—in a government database. To see these

CURING CONCUSSION?

In 2012 and 2013, the FDA identified three companies marketing numerous dietary supplements that claimed to cure or prevent concussions and other serious traumatic brain injuries. Medical experts are only now learning how to best treat patients with such brain injuries. False assurances of recovery may convince athletes, coaches, and parents that a person who has had a concussion is ready to return to play. Returning to sports too soon after a concussion can be very dangerous. The FDA says no dietary supplement can cure a concussion.

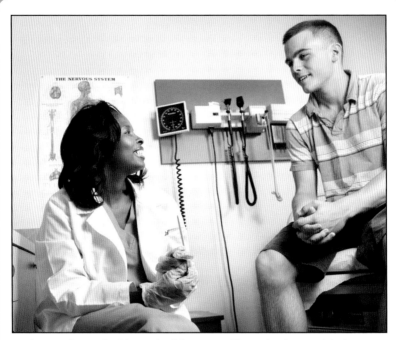

For best results, work with your health-care provider to develop a weight-loss or athletic program.

reports, submit a Freedom of Information Act request to the FDA in writing or online at http://www.fda.gov/RegulatoryInformation/FOI/HowToMakeaFOIArequest/default.htm.

Remember, dietary supplements are not intended to prevent, treat, or cure a disease or condition. However, in certain cases and for certain people, a dietary supplement taken with a doctor's advice is appropriate. Always work with your health-care provider to develop a plan to reach optimal health. Dietary supplements may be part of that plan. More often they are not.

Some supplements will help some people some of the time, even in the absence of scientific evidence. Whether you believe dietary supplements are harmless, helpful, or hurtful, you need to be aware of their benefits and potential risks.

DO IT RIGHT: SAFE INTERNET SEARCHES

When searching for information about dietary supplements on the Internet, ask yourself these questions:

1. Who operates the site? Is it the FDA or the National Institutes of Health or another reputable government source? Is it a university such as the Johns Hopkins University School of Medicine? A health-care center such as the Mayo Clinic or a well-known nonprofit association such as the American Heart Association or the American Diabetes Association? If the URL extension is not .gov or .org or .edu, dig deeper and look instead for more reliable, trustworthy information elsewhere.

2. What is the purpose of the site? Is it to educate the public or to sell a product? Most government and nonprofit organization sites do not contain advertising. Approach with caution any site that is focused only on promoting a product for profit.

3. What is the source of the information, and does it contain verifiable references? Did recognized experts write the information? The full name and the title of the authors should be included on the site. Has the information been published in reputable scientific and professional journals? If so, this is an indicator of reliable information. Personal testimonials and success stories scattered around a website, on the other hand, are a red flag that the information may not be based on scientific evidence.

4. Is the information current? Check the date the material was posted or updated. Researchers make new discoveries every day. Don't rely on outdated information.

GLOSSARY

AEGELINE: a substance naturally occurring in the bael fruit tree. It was found in a weight-loss supplement that caused liver failure in some people who took it. The FDA forced the product off the market in 2013.

AMINO ACIDS: chemicals the body uses to build proteins. They are found naturally in foods that contain protein, such as meat, poultry, fish, and beans.

ANABOLIC-ANDROGENIC STEROIDS (AAS): synthetic chemicals similar to the hormone testosterone, which males produce naturally. The anabolic effects of AAS build muscle and increase strength. The androgenic effects enhance secondary male sexual characteristics. AAS are very dangerous and are illegal in the United States without a doctor's prescription.

BLOOD DOPING: an illegal process that some athletes use to improve their performance. Blood doping increases the number of red blood cells that carry oxygen, thereby improving athletic endurance and performance. It may include blood transfusions, injection of erythropoietin, or use of synthetic oxygen carriers.

BRANCHED-CHAIN AMINO ACIDS: three amino acids (leucine, isoleucine, and valine) used as sports supplements. They may reduce muscle breakdown during exercise but are unlikely to improve overall athletic performance.

CARBOHYDRATE: one of three macronutrients. Carbohydrates provide energy and are found naturally in many foods such as grains, fruits, and vegetables.

CONTAMINANTS: substances accidentally or purposefully added to a product at the factory during production or packaging. They may include pesticides, traces of other products (such as walnuts or penicillin), and prescription drugs. Manufacturers do not list such substances on the supplement label.

CREATINE: a widely used, legal amino acid that may help athletic performance for the first few minutes of high-intensity exercise

DEHYDROEPIANDROSTERONE (DHEA): a hormone the body naturally converts to testosterone. Some dietary supplements contain this ingredient. Organizations such as the National Collegiate Athletic Association and the US Anti-Doping Agency have banned its use by athletes.

DETOXIFICATION: cleansing the body of poisons. Supplements and other products taken to cleanse the body are useless and may be dangerous. The human body is fully capable of detoxifying itself with organs such as the liver, kidneys, and lungs.

DIETARY SUPPLEMENT: an ingredient added to a diet that supplements but does not replace food. They include vitamins, minerals, herbs, and amino acids. Users who take supplements typically do so in the belief it will improve health or athletic performance or that it will help them to lose weight and to have more energy.

DIETARY SUPPLEMENT HEALTH AND EDUCATION ACT (DSHEA): an act passed by the US Congress in 1994 to recategorize dietary supplements as food products rather than medications. As such, the FDA has regulatory authority only after the product is for sale. Under DSHEA, the company that makes a dietary supplement is responsible for ensuring its safety during the development and manufacturing processes.

DIMETHYLAMYLAMINE (DMAA): a powerful stimulant taken as a sports supplement. The product is banned in the United States. Its side effects are similar to those of amphetamine (speed) and include chest pain, breathing problems, and seizures.

DISCLAIMER: a statement of explanation on dietary supplement labels that says the FDA has not evaluated the claims made by the supplement manufacturer. This disclaimer is required by law in the United States on all dietary supplements.

EPHEDRA: a once-popular weight-loss herb. In 2004 the FDA banned the sale of ephedra in the United States because of serious side effects.

ERGOGENIC AIDS: another term for sports supplements

FAT: one of three macronutrients. Fats provide energy, help vitamin absorption, and insulate the body. They come from animal products such as meat and butter and from some plants such as nuts and avocados.

FOOD AND DRUG ADMINISTRATION (FDA): a US government organization charged with ensuring the safety and effectiveness of prescription and over-the-counter drugs in the United States. The FDA has limited oversight of the dietary supplement industry. The FDA randomly tests products, collects reports of adverse effects from consumers and health-care providers, and can require a manufacturer to recall dangerous products.

HERBS: the leaves, flowers, seeds, berries, bark, and roots of plants and trees. Herbal medicines made from plants have been used around the world to treat medical conditions for at least five thousand years. Some of them, such as the foxglove plant, have been synthesized and turned into effective and legitimate prescription medications. Others are dangerous and should be strictly avoided.

HUMAN CHORIONIC GONADOTROPIN (HCG): a hormone that women produce naturally during pregnancy and that is used illegally as a weight-loss product

MACRONUTRIENTS: carbohydrates, fats, and proteins. These sources of natural body fuel have the calories that give us energy and promote growth.

MICRONUTRIENTS: vitamins and minerals. The body needs only small amounts of micronutrients to regulate our metabolism and assist in many bodily processes.

MINERALS: naturally occurring substances such as calcium and iron that come from nonliving sources. Humans ingest minerals through plant-based foods that pick up minerals from the soil in which they grow or from the meat of animals that eat those plants. Minerals help regulate many bodily systems such as growth, digestion, the immune system, and energy production. The human body requires only small amounts of these micronutrients.

PROTEIN: one of three macronutrients. Proteins help to build and maintain the human body by building muscle mass, strengthening the immune system, and repairing damaged cells. Good sources of protein include meat, nuts, fish, eggs, milk, and certain vegetables such as beans.

RECOMMENDED DIETARY ALLOWANCE (RDA): the recommended daily amount of a nutrient sufficient to meet the requirements of 97 to 98 percent of healthy people. The RDA varies by age and gender and is set by the FDA.

SPORTS SUPPLEMENTS: dietary supplements taken for the purpose of building muscles, improving stamina, and speeding up recovery time. Many are dangerous and are banned in sports competition.

STIMULANTS: chemicals such as 1,3-dimethylamylamine (DMAA) that speed up the body's central nervous system. Many of the sports supplements sold as stimulants include amphetamine- and methamphetamine-like substances or substances the body turns into amphetamine and methamphetamine. Most of these are illegal, and all are dangerous.

VITAMINS: substances that come from animals and plants and that are found naturally in all foods. They help regulate many bodily systems and functions including growth, digestion, the immune system, and energy production. The human body requires only small amounts of these micronutrients.

WEIGHT-LOSS SUPPLEMENTS: dietary supplements taken for the purpose of aiding weight loss. Many of these supplements come from plants. Some are dangerous, while others lead to only temporary weight loss.

SOURCE NOTES

4   "Supplements: Nutrition in a Pill?," Mayo Clinic, accessed October 14, 2014, http://www.mayoclinic.org/healthy -living/nutrition-and-healthy-eating/in-depth/ supplements/art-20044894.

4   Maggie DeWolfe, "I Regret Not Loving Myself Sooner," *The Gloss* (blog), accessed September 14, 2014, http://www .thegloss.com/2012/05/04/beauty/i-regret-not-loving -myself-sooner-378/.

4–5   Maggie DeWolfe, "Crash Diet Horror Story: I Hallucinated Cats," *The Gloss* (blog), accessed September 14, 2014, http:// www.thegloss.com/2011/12/13/beauty/crash-diet-horror -story-i-hallucinated-cats-413/.

5   Dr. Paul M. Coates, "Message from the Director," Office of Dietary Supplements, NIH, accessed September 27, 2014, http://ods.od.nih.gov/About/Message_from_the_Director .aspx.

6   Annette Dickinson and Douglas MacKay, "Health Habits and Other Characteristics of Dietary Supplement Users: A Review," *Nutrition Journal* 13 (2014): 14, http://www.nutritionj.com /content/13/1/14.

9   "Code of Federal Regulations Title 21—Food Labeling," FDA, accessed September 13, 2014, http://www.accessdata.fda .gov/scripts/cdrh/cfdocs/cfcfr/CFRSearch.cfm?fr=101.93.

9   Pieter A Cohen, "Hazards of Hindsight—Monitoring the Safety of Nutritional Supplements," *New England Journal of Medicine* 370 (2014), accessed September 20, 2014, http://www.nejm .org/doi/full/10.1056/NEJMp1315559.

9-10   Michael Carome, quoted in Tammie Smith, "Regulations Differ for Supplements," *Richmond Times Dispatch*, July 21, 2013, http://www.timesdispatch.com/news/local/regulations -differ-for-supplements/article_45dda9ae-b755-5ddb-8e62

-35f58ab4facb.html.

11   "The NSF Mark," NSF, accessed November 3, 2014, http://
        www.nsf.org/about-nsf/nsf-mark/.

11   "USP Verification Services FAQs," U.S. Pharmacopeial
        Convention, accessed November 3, 2014, http://www
        .usp.org/support-home/frequently-asked-questions/usp
        -verification-services.

12   Jill Koegel, "6 Tips to Speed Up Your Body Naturally without
        Supplements," *Live Well Nebraska*, October 23, 2013, http://
        www.livewellnebraska.com/nutrition/tips-to-speed-up-your
        -body-naturally-without-supplements/article_85240df7
        -d57e-5326-a072-d28be8fd90fb.html.

13   Dale Ames Kline, personal interview with the author, January
        16, 2014.

13   Mandy Martin, quoted in "How One Woman Lost 50+ Pounds,"
        Women'sHealth, July 16, 2013, http://www
        .womenshealthmag.com/weight-loss/diets-that-work.

13   Ibid.

14   Ibid.

14   "Childhood Obesity Facts," CDC, accessed September 15, 2014,
        http://www.cdc.gov/healthyyouth/obesity/facts.htm.

20   Nancy Clark, personal interview with the author, April 2,
        2014.

20   Cindy Cotte Griffiths, "Struggling with a Severe Vitamin
        D Deficiency," *Trying Not to Bneg* (blog), January 8, 2012,
        http://www.tryingnottobneg.com/?s=vitamin+d.

20   Ibid.

21   Ibid.

22   "Metabolism and Weight Loss: How You Burn Calories," Mayo
        Clinic, accessed September 16, 2014, http://www.mayoclinic

.org/healthy-living/weight-loss/in-depth/metabolism/art
-20046508.

26   Guallar Eliseo, Saverio Stranges, Cynthia Mulrow, Lawrence J. Appel, and Edgar R. Miller III, "Enough Is Enough: Stop Wasting Money on Vitamin and Mineral Supplements," *Annals of Internal Medicine* 159, no. 12 (2013): 850–851, accessed September 28, 2014, http://annals.org/article .aspx?articleid=1789253.

27   Kline, interview.

28   Herbert Bonkovsky, quoted in, "Featured Research: Liver Dangers from Herbal Supplements, OTC and RX Drugs, New Guidelines Warn," *Science Daily*, June 17, 2014, http://www .sciencedaily.com/releases/2014/06/140617091738.htm.

28   Karen Schlendorf, quoted in "Herbal Warning," *Newsweek*, May 5, 1996, http://www.newsweek.com/herbal -warning-178356.

35   Murray Feingold, quoted in, "Herbal Supplemental Use Is Controversial," *MetroWest Daily News* (Framingham, MA), December 3, 2013, http://www.metrowestdailynews.com /article/20131203/News/312039906.

36   Diana Wright, personal interview with the author, April 14, 2014.

36   Anahad O'Connor, "Spike in Harm to Liver Is Tied to Dietary Aids," *New York Times*, December 21, 2013, http://www .nytimes.com/2013/12/22/us/spike-in-harm-to-liver-is-tied -to-dietary-aids.html?_r=4&adxnnl=1&adxnnlx=1387825792 -rBP9oo6sBuHFOjrbNpRvTA&.

38   Wright, interview.

43   Pieter Cohen, quoted in Angela Haupt, "HCG Diet Dangers: Is Fast Weight Loss Worth the Risk?," *U.S. News*, March 14, 2011, http://health.usnews.com/health-news/diet-fitness/diet /articles/2011/03/14/hcg-diet-dangers-is-fast-weight-loss

-worth-the-risk.

43–44   "Raspberry Ketone Based Supplement Helps Weight Loss,"
        foodconsumer.org, December 29, 2013, http://www
        .foodconsumer.org/newsite/Nutrition/Supplements
        /raspberry_ketone_weight_loss_1229131129.html.

47   Wright, interview.

48   Trevor Gillum, personal interview with the author, January
        17, 2014.

50   Trevor Gillum, personal interview with the author, September
        22, 2014.

51   Ibid.

53   Gillum, interview, January 17, 2014.

55–56   Pieter Cohen, quoted in "NSF International Discovers
        Emerging and Potentially Harmful Adulterant in Dietary
        Supplements," press release, NSF, October 14, 2013, http://
        www.nsf.org/newsroom/emerging-and-potentially-harmful
        -adulterant-depea-found-in-supplements.

56   Victor Navarro, quoted in "Hepatotoxicity from Bodybuilding
        Supplements Rising," Medscape, November 6, 2013, http://
        www.medscape.com/viewarticle/813906.

56   Clark, interview.

58   Tyson Gay, quoted in David Epstein, "Cheat Sheet: The Tyson
        Gay File," Sports Illustrated, February 10, 2014, http://
        sportsillustrated.cnn.com/more/news/20140210/tyson-gay
        -failed-drug-test/#ixzz2x6AZ53pU.

60   Lance Armstrong, quoted in Russell Goldman, "Lance
        Armstrong Admits to Doping," ABC News, January 17, 2014,
        http://abcnews.go.com/US/lance-armstrong-confesses
        -doping/story?id=18244003&singlePage=true.

61   "Bud Selig Says Alex Rodriguez Will Have a Clean Slate after
        Serving PED Suspension," NY Daily News, September 23, 2014,

http://www.nydailynews.com/sports/baseball/yankees
/bud-selig-alex-rodriguez-clean-slate-serving-ped
-suspension-article-1.1950369.

61 Alex Rodriguez, in Steve Fishman, "Chasing A-Rod," *New York Magazine*, December 1, 2013, http://nymag.com/news /sports/alex-rodriguez-2013-12/.

62 Amy Eichner, quoted in Natasha Singer and Peter Lattman, "Is the Seller to Blame?," *New York Times*, March 15, 2013, http:// www.nytimes.com/2013/03/17/business/a-soldiers -parents-take-aim-at-gnc-and-a-supplement-maker.html? _r=0.

63 Gary Coody, quoted in "6 Tip-Offs to Rip-Offs: Don't Fall for Health Fraud Scams," FDA, accessed November 4, 2014, http://www.fda.gov/forconsumers/consumerupdates /ucm341344.htm.

63 Teresa Cantwell, quoted in Delthia Ricks, "FDA Official: 70% of Supplement Companies Violate Agency Rules," *Newsday .com*, August 23, 2013, http://www.newsday.com/news /health/fda-official-70-of-supplement-companies-violate -agency-rules-1.5920525.

65 Steven G. Newmaster, Meghan Grguric, Dhivya Shanmughanandhan, Sathishkumar Ramalingam, and Subramanyam Ragupathy, "DNA Barcoding Detects Contamination and Substitution in North American Herbal Products," *BMC Medicine* 11 (2013): 222, accessed September 26, 2014, http://www.biomedcentral.com/1741 -7015/11/222.

66 Gillum, interview, January 17, 2014.

67 Frank Sacks, quoted in "The Truth about Detox Diets," *WebMD*, November 4, 2014, http://www.webmd.com/diet /detox-diets.

SELECTED BIBLIOGRAPHY

Bailey, Regan L., Jaime J. Gahche, Paige E. Miller, Paul R. Thomas, and Johanna T. Dwyer. "Why US Adults Use Dietary Supplements." *JAMA Internal Medicine* 173, no. 5 (March 11, 2013) : 355–361. http://archinte.jamanetwork.com/article.aspx?articleid=1568520.

Bent, S. "Herbal Medicine in the United States: Review of Efficacy, Safety, and Regulation." *Journal of General Internal Medicine* 23, no. 6 (June 2008): 854–859. Accessed September 28, 2004. http://www.ncbi.nlm.nih.gov/pmc/articles/PMC2517879/.

Booth, J. N., S. D. Leary, C. Joinson, A. R. Ness, P. D. Tomporowski, J. M. Boyle, and J. J. Reilly. "Associations between Objectively Measured Physical Activity and Academic Attainment in Adolescents from a UK Cohort." *British Journal of Sports Medicine* 48 (2014): 265–270. Accessed September 28, 2014. http://bjsm.bmj.com/content/48/3/265.full.

Dickinson, Annette, and Douglas MacKay. "Health Habits and Other Characteristics of Dietary Supplement Users." *Nutrition Journal* 13 (2014): 14. Accessed September 28, 2014. http://www.nutritionj.com/content/13/1/14.

Eisenberg, Maria E., Melanie Wall, and Dianne Neumark-Sztainer. "Muscle-Enhancing Behaviors among Adolescent Girls and Boys." *Pediatrics* 130, no. 6 (December 2012): 1019–1026. Accessed September 28, 2014. http://www.ncbi.nlm.nih.gov/pmc/articles/PMC3507247/.

Epstein, David. "Cheat Sheet: The Tyson Gay File." *ProPublica*, May 2, 2014. http://www.propublica.org/article/cheat-sheet-the-tyson-gay-file.

Evans, Marion Willard, Jr., Harrison Ndetan, Michael Perko,

Ronald Williams, and Clark Walker. "Dietary Supplement Use by Children and Adolescents in the United States to Enhance Sport Performance." *Journal of Primary Prevention* 33, no. 1 (2012): 3–12. Accessed September 28, 2014. http://www.medscape.com /viewarticle/759015.

Fakhouri, Tala H. I., Jeffery P. Hughes, Vicki L. Burt, MinKyoung Song, Janet E. Fulton, and Cynthia L. Ogden. "Physical Activity in US Youth Aged 12–15 Years, 2012." *NCHS Data Brief*, no. 141, January 2014. Centers for Disease Control and Prevention. Accessed September 28, 2014. http://www.cdc.gov/nchs/data/databriefs /db141.htm.

 "Food Groups." ChooseMyPlate.gov. Accessed September 28, 2014. http://www.choosemyplate.gov/food-groups/.

Guallar Eliseo, Saverio Stranges, Cynthia Mulrow, Lawrence J. Appel, and Edgar R. Miller III. "Enough Is Enough: Stop Wasting Money on Vitamin and Mineral Supplements." *Annals of Internal Medicine* 159, no. 12 (2013): 850–851. Accessed September 28, 2014. http:// annals.org/article.aspx?articleid=1789253.

"Gut Check: A Reference Guide for Media on Spotting False Weight Loss Claims." Federal Trade Commission. Accessed September 28, 2014. http://www.business.ftc.gov/documents/0492-gut-check -reference-guide-media-spotting-false-weight-loss-claims.

Hiltzik, Michael. "Dietary Supplements: The Deadly Toll of Deregulation." *Los Angeles Times*, April 9, 2014. http://www. latimes.com/business/hiltzik/la-fi-mh-herbal -supplements-20140409,0,696905.column#axzz2yV3Ms2Re.

Jones, William. *Performance Eating*. New York: iUniverse, 2006.

"Label Claims for Conventional Foods and Dietary Supplements." Food and Drug Administration. December 2013. Accessed June 2,

2014. http://www.fda.gov/food/ingredientspackaginglabeling
/labelingnutrition/ucm111447.htm.

"Managing Media: We Need a Plan." Press release. American
Academy of Pediatrics. October 28, 2013. http://www.aap.org
/en-us/about-the-aap/aap-press-room/pages/Managing-Media
-We-Need-a-Plan.aspx.

Newmaster, Steven G., Meghan Grguric, Dhivya
Shanmughanandhan, Sathishkumar Ramalingam, and
Subramanyam Ragupathy. "DNA Barcoding Detects Contamination
and Substitution in North American Herbal Products." *BMC Medicine*
11 (2013): 222. Accessed September 28, 2014. http://www.
biomedcentral.com/1741-7015/11/222.

"Q&A on Dietary Supplements." Food and Drug Administration.
Accessed September 28, 2014. http://www.fda.gov/Food
/DietarySupplements/QADietarySupplements/default.htm.

Ricks, Delthia. "FDA Official: 70% of Supplement Companies Violate
Agency Rules." *Newsday*, August 23, 2013. http://www.newsday
.com/news/health/fda-official-70-of-supplement-companies
-violate-agency-rules-1.5920525.

"6 Tip-Offs to Rip-Offs: Don't Fall for Health Fraud Scams." FDA.
Accessed September 28, 2014. http://www.fda.gov/forconsumers
/consumerupdates/ucm341344.htm.

"Sports Supplements." TeensHealth.org from Nemours. Accessed
September 28, 2014. http://kidshealth.org/teen/food_fitness
/sports/sports_supplements.html#.

"Supplements for Weight Loss." *WebMD*. Accessed September 28,
2014. http://www.webmd.com/vitamins-and-supplements
/lifestyle-guide-11/diet-weight-loss-supplements?page=1.

"Tips for Dietary Supplement Users." Food and Drug Administration. Accessed September 28, 2014. http://www.fda.gov/Food /DietarySupplements/UsingDietarySupplements/ucm110567.htm.

"Using Dietary Supplements Wisely." National Center for Complementary and Alternative Medicine. Accessed June 2, 2014. http://nccam.nih.gov/health/supplements/wiseuse.htm.

FOR FURTHER INFORMATION

BOOKS

Albergotti, Reed, and Vanessa O'Connell. *Wheelmen: Lance Armstrong, the Tour de France, and the Greatest Sports Conspiracy Ever.* New York: Dutton, 2013. Written by *Wall Street Journal* reporters, this book tells the story of how cyclist Lance Armstrong and his team perpetrated one of the greatest conspiracies in the history of sports.

Berlatsky, Noah. *Dietary Supplements.* Opposing Viewpoints series. Farmington Hills, MI: Greenhaven Press, 2014. This teen book offers a selection of articles by experts that examine the pros and cons of using dietary supplements.

Clark, Nancy. *Nancy Clark's Sports Nutrition Guidebook.* 5th ed. Champaign, IL: Human Kinetics, 2013. This book for teens and adults provides extensive information about everyday eating, the science of eating and exercise, balancing weight and activity, and healthy recipes.

Cooper, Chris. *Run, Swim, Throw, Cheat: The Science behind Drugs in Sport.* Oxford: Oxford University Press, 2012. Cooper's book examines how athletes have cheated by using illegal performance-enhancing drugs and how they will likely continue to do so. He explores the science behind blood doping and performance-enhancing drugs.

Davis, Catherine G. *Alternative Medicine*. Minneapolis: Twenty-First Century Books, 2012. Written for young adults, Davis's book explores alternatives to traditional medical care, including herbal remedies, acupuncture, meditation, and yoga.

Mueller, Kimberly, and Josh Hingst. T*he Athlete's Guide to Sports Supplements*. Champaign, IL: Human Kinetics, 2013. Primarily for adults, this book describes 120 commonly used supplements. Each entry explains how the supplement works, its potential benefits, research studies and outcomes, and possible health concerns.

Shanley, Ellen, and Colleen Thompson. *Fueling the Teen Machine*. Boulder, CO: Bull, 2011. For teens and adults, this book covers essential facts about general nutrition, weight management, exercise, eating disorders, vegetarianism, and sports nutrition.

VIDEOS

Cycling's Greatest Fraud: Lance Armstrong National Geographic Documentary. YouTube video, 45:00. Created by National Geographic. Posted by "gambit102." March 26, 2014. https://www.youtube.com /watch?v=PgRBxsW26vY. This film documents the science and scheming behind Lance Armstrong and his cycling team, called the most sophisticated and successful doping scheme in all of sports.

"FDA Basic Video: Vasilios H. Frankos Discusses Dietary Supplements." Food and Drug Administration, 8:32. Last modified April 11, 2014. http://www.fda.gov/AboutFDA/Transparency/Basics/ucm195691. htm. The former director of the Center for Food Safety and Applied Nutrition discusses the FDA's role in monitoring dietary supplements.

"Lance Armstrong Oprah Interview: Doping Confession to Winfrey after Years of Denial." YouTube video, 3:17. Posted by "ABC News." January 18, 2013. https://www.youtube.com/watch?v=ZxkULBtpF3s. This is an excerpt from Lance Armstrong's live television interview with Oprah Winfrey in which he confesses to years of illegal drug use and blood doping.

Losing It: The Big Fat Trap. Promises, Promises. Five Die after Lap-Band Surgery. *ABC News*, May 12, 2012. http://abcnews.go.com/2020 /video/losing-big-fat-trap-16331564?tab=9482930&section=120686 3&playlist=16332677. This series of short videos highlights celebrity weight-loss successes and failures, yo-yo dieting, and more.

Nutritional Supplements. YouTube video, 49:07. BBC documentary. Posted by "healthinformationonline.info." December 16, 2013. https://www.youtube.com/watch?v=0tZLg-WIQCs. Filmed in the United Kingdom and the United States, this documentary examines the truth and myths behind vitamin usage, explains vitamins' role as antioxidants, and discusses how supplements caused some cases of cancer and liver diseases.

ORGANIZATIONS

Academy of Nutrition and Dietetics
120 South Riverside Plaza, Suite 2000
Chicago, IL 60606
(800) 877-1600
http://www.eatright.org
The Academy of Nutrition and Dietetics strives to improve the nation's
health and advance the profession of dietetics through research,
education, and advocacy. The organization's website contains a wealth
of nutrition information and is an excellent source for accurate food
and nutrition information.

American College of Sports Medicine
401 West Michigan St.
Indianapolis, IN 46202
(317) 637-9200
http://www.acsm.org/access-public-information
The American College of Sports Medicine is the largest sports medicine
and exercise science organization in the world. More than fifty
thousand international, national, and regional members and certified
professionals are dedicated to advancing and integrating scientific
research to provide educational and practical applications of exercise
science and sports medicine.

ChooseMyPlate.gov
USDA Center for Nutrition Policy and Promotion
3101 Park Center Dr.
Alexandria, VA 22302-1594
http://www.choosemyplate.gov/
The USDA Center for Nutrition Policy and Promotion focuses on two
primary objectives. These are to advance and promote dietary guidance
for all Americans and to research and analyze nutrition and consumer
economics. The USDA released MyPlate in 2011, an icon with the intent
to prompt consumers to think about building a healthy plate at each
meal.

Food and Drug Administration (FDA)
10903 New Hampshire Ave.
Silver Spring, MD 20993
(888) 463-6332
http://www.fda.gov/Food/DietarySupplements/default.htm
The FDA works to ensure the safety, effectiveness, and security of human drugs, vaccines, and other biological products for human use. It tracks complaints about dietary supplements and randomly tests them. The FDA also has the authority to force a manufacturer to recall a dangerous product. This section offers a Q&A section, tips on safe use of dietary supplements, and more.

International Olympic Committee (IOC)
Château de Vidy
Case postale 356
1001 Lausanne, Switzerland
http://www.olympic.org/about-ioc-institution
The IOC is the supreme authority of the Olympic Games. On its website, the IOC states that its functions include the following: "To encourage and support the promotion of ethics in sport; to lead the fight against doping in sport; to encourage and support measures protecting the health of athletes; and to encourage and support the organization, development and coordination of sport and sports competitions." The website includes information on how drug testing is performed on Olympic athletes.

National Center for Complementary and Alternative Medicine (NCCAM)
31 Center Dr., MSC 2182
Bethesda, MD 20892
(888) 644-6226
http://nccam.nih.gov/health/supplements/wiseuse.htm
NCCAM's mission is "to define, through rigorous scientific investigation, the usefulness and safety of complementary and alternative medicine interventions (including dietary supplements) and their roles in improving health and health care." The section on using supplements wisely offers extensive resources including key points about dietary supplements, how they are regulated, safety considerations, and links to further research.

Nutrition.gov
Dietary Supplements
Food and Nutrition Information Center
10301 Baltimore Ave.
Beltsville, MD 20705-2351
http://www.nutrition.gov/dietary-supplements
This site provides easy access to vetted food and nutrition information
from agencies of the US federal government. It serves as a gateway
to reliable information on nutrition, healthy eating, physical activity,
and food safety for consumers. The section on dietary supplements is
extensive and offers detailed information about herbal supplements,
vitamins and minerals, and supplements used by athletes.

Office of Dietary Supplements (ODS)
National Institutes of Health
6100 Executive Blvd., Room 3B01, MSC 7517
Bethesda, MD 20892-7517
(301) 435-2920
http://ods.od.nih.gov/
The mission of ODS is to "strengthen knowledge and understanding of
dietary supplements by evaluating scientific information, stimulating
and supporting research, disseminating research results, and educating
the public to foster an enhanced quality of life and health for the U.S.
population." The website provides detailed information sheets for
dozens of supplements, including vitamins, minerals, and botanical
products.

U.S. Anti-Doping Agency (USADA)
5555 Tech Center Dr., Suite 200
Colorado Springs, CO 80919
(719) 785-2000
http://www.usantidoping.org/
The USADA's mission is "to preserve competitive integrity, inspire true
sport, and to protect the rights of US Olympic and Paralympic athletes.
It provides education, research, and testing for banned substances."
The website allows users to determine if a legitimate prescription
medication includes banned substances (some do) and describes the
dangers of PEDs in detail.

INDEX

PHOTO ACKNOWLEDGMENTS

The images in this book are used with the permission of: Backgrounds: © iStockphoto.com/Tuned_In © Mike Kemp/RubberBall/Alamy, p. 1 (spoon); © iStockphoto.com/diane39, p. 7; U.S. Food and Drug Administration, p. 8; Courtesy of Consumer Lab, p. 11 (top); NSF International via Wikipedia, p. 11 (middle); The U.S. Pharmacopeial Convention (USP), p. 11 (bottom); Agricultural Research Service, USDA, p. 16; © iStockphoto.com/skynesher, p. 19; © iStockphoto.com/mcfields, p. 22; © Elena Elisseeva/Alamy, p. 30; © Universal Images Group/Getty Images, p. 31; © Blend Images/Alamy, p. 37; © iStockphoto.com/Brasil2, p. 38; © Thecrossroads/Dreamstime.com, p. 40; © Ekkapon Sriharun/Alamy, p. 41; © iStockphoto.com/langdu, p. 42; © iStockphoto.com/AvalonStudio_WojciechKryczka, p. 43; © Tim Robbins/Mint Images/Getty Images, p. 46; © Heather Angel/Natural Visions/Alamy, p. 49; © Joel Ford/Getty Images, p. 49; © iStockphoto.com/celsopupo, p. 52; © Ingram Publishing/E+/Getty Images, p. 54; AP Photo/Dave Thompson/PA Wire, p. 58; © Jaime Reina/AFP/Getty Images, p. 59; © Leon Halip/Getty Images, p. 61; © Mark Elias/Bloomberg/Getty Images, p. 65; © Camille Tokerud/Iconica/Getty Images, p. 70.

Front cover: © Cultura Science/Rafe Swan/Oxford Scientific/Getty Images.

Back cover and flaps: © iStockphoto.com/Tuned_In.

ABOUT THE AUTHOR

Connie Goldsmith has written fifteen nonfiction books for middle-school and upper-grade readers, mostly on health topics, and has also published more than two hundred magazine articles for adults and children. She is an active member of the Society of Children's Book Writers and Illustrators and of the Authors Guild. Goldsmith is also a registered nurse with a bachelor of science degree in nursing and a master of public administration degree in health care. Additionally, Goldsmith writes for nurses and writes a child health column for a regional parenting magazine in Sacramento, California, where she lives.

AUTHOR ACKNOWLEDGMENTS

The author wishes to thank the following individuals for their contributions to this work:

Nancy Clark, MS, RD, CSSD (dietitian, sports nutrition counselor, author, member of the American Academy of Sports Medicine, and private practitioner in the Boston, Massachusetts, area)

Trevor Gillum, PhD, assistant professor, Department of Kinesiology, California Baptist University (exercise physiologist)

Dale Ames Kline, MS, RD, LD (dietitian, author, and director of Food, Nutrition and Dietetics for Gannett Education)

Diana Wright, PhD, RD (dietitian, nutrition educator, adjunct community college faculty, and corporate wellness provider)